DEDICATION

This book is humbly dedicated to those lovers of the truth who refused to believe the carefully contrived lie about the so-called "Incredible Mis-Trial"; and to the prospect that *truth* will prove to be a dynamic and moving force to correct that incredible *lie* being promoted and taught even in the best of Christian colleges, seminaries and publications.

JACOB GARTENHAUS, D.D., Litt.D., L.L.D.

Author of . . .

Winning Jews to Christ 2.50
Unto His Own (Same as above, paperback) . . 1.50
The Jew and Jesus Christ 50

And the following tracts . . .

Who Is He? 10
How to Win the Jews 10
Come Now, and Let Us Reason 10
Remarkable Story of Dr. Kurt Weiss 10

(Order of 25 or More, 5c Each)

◊

The books below are being prepared for publication:

Anti-Semitism and Christianity
Judaizing: An Old Threat Renewed
The Trinity
The Ten Lost Tribes: Who Are They?
etc.

◊

Published By

Box 3307   •   Chattanooga, Tenn. 37404

THE "CHRIST-KILLERS"
Past and Present

By

JACOB GARTENHAUS, D.D., Litt.D., L.L.D.

HEBREW CHRISTIAN PRESS

Contents

Foreword

I have read the galley proofs of this remarkable book—CHRIST KILLERS. In doing so I was like a diver plunging down in deep waters to pearl beds—and when the diver came up with both hands full of pearls, he left more pearls behind than he brought up.

This is one of the most intensely interesting and unusually unique books of the hundreds of books I have read in my life.

This book makes the reader give thought to questions and answers given about Jesus and Gentiles as their words and deeds are related to the crucifixion of Jesus Christ.

The author says that to argue who killed Christ is theological nonsense and spiritual insanity. And the author, with wisdom and certainty, gives seven propositions which are contrary to current widely-accepted notions.

In this book, Jesus is set forth as the criticized Christ who spoke severe criticisms against the hypocrites among the rulers, the elders, the Scribes, Pharisees, and Sadducees—and against their abuse of their authority in society by dominating and suppressing the common people.

This book asks and answers such questions as "Did the Jews reject Christ?" "Did the Jews crucify Christ?" "Was the Jewish court trial illegal?" "Is the New Testament anti-semitic?" "Do Hebrew Christians cease to be Jews?"

To all who will read this unique book, with all its statements Scripturally fortified, it will prove to be a wonderful book full of wonders—really.

To all who would like to know more of the matter of Christ's life and crucifixion as they are related to the Jews and Gentiles, this book is an invaluable treasure. I believe that all who read this remarkably unique book will be made wiser—and better.

The climax of the whole matter is not WHO but WHAT killed Jesus. The answer is our SINS—yes, OUR sins.

ROBERT G. LEE, Ph.D., D.D.

Introduction

Dr. Jacob Gartenhaus' book, *Christ-Killers: Past and Present,* is one of the most powerful arguments I have ever read on one of the greatest and most bitterly contested and divisive issues in history: the responsibility of the Jews for the crucifixion of Jesus Christ.

Dr. Gartenhaus, appealing to the record in the Four Gospels and the history, ancient and modern, of Gentile unbelief in, and opposition to, Jesus Christ, argues that the Jews were no more responsible for the crucifixion than the Gentiles.

" 'Who killed Christ?'—We should ask 'What killed Christ?' The answer, of course, would be 'OUR Sins.' "

A court of law hears arguments on both sides of an issue, and said court gives careful consideration to arguments on both sides. Dr. Gartenhaus is arguing his case before the bar of public opinion. His argument deserves a serious and respectful hearing, and fair-minded people will accord it to him. He asks nothing more.

Jew-haters never make a distinction between believing and unbelieving Jews in the days of Christ, in the Book of Acts, or in succeeding ages. They make no distinction between good Jews and bad Jews.

Jew-haters never have anything to say about these unchallenged facts:

That every book in the Bible was written by Jews with the exception of two, Luke and Acts; that John the Baptist was a Jew; that Jesus Christ was a Jew; that all the apostles were Jews; that the first to follow Christ and the first to die for Him were Jews; that Bethlehem was a Jewish village; that Calvary was a Jewish hill; that the empty tomb was a Jewish tomb in a Jewish garden, and that He ascended from a Jewish village, Bethany.

And that Pentecost is a Jewish term. The 120 followers of Christ assembled in the Jewish city of Jerusalem on that wonderful day were all Jews. The preacher who preached the sermon on that day was a Jew. The 3,000 souls converted on that day were all Jews. The "Mother

Church" was 100 per cent Jewish. The first missionaries were Jews and the first martyrs were Jews.

We are constantly speaking of the apostolic churches in that flaming Book of Acts. Every church mentioned in the Book of Acts was founded by Jews. As to the church at Rome, on the day of Pentecost Jews were present from Rome (Acts 2:10). It is more probable that these Jews went back to Rome and founded a church than it is that the church was founded by pagan Gentiles.

What is the Book of Acts but the Divine record of Jewish missions in that first century?

The Jew-haters are constantly telling us that Karl Marx was a Jew; that the old scoundrel was the father of communism, and therefore the Jews are the real founders of communism and are originally responsible for communism.

But these anti-Semites never have a word to say about the following unchallenged facts:

That Karl Marx's parents professed the Protestant religion; that Karl Marx's intimate friends were not Jews in Jerusalem but Gentiles in the Doctors' club in Berlin; that Karl Marx married Jenny von Westphalen, the daughter of the Royal Prussian privy Councillor Ludwig von Westphalen.

And these anti-Semites don't tell you that no man of his day hated Jews and Negroes more than Karl Marx, and that no man of his day wrote more mean and dirty things about them than did Karl Marx. Listen to Otto Ruhle in his "Karl Marx: His Life and Work" (The New Home Library, New York):

"Very striking is the unusual acerbity with which, when he is discussing the Jewish problem, Marx attacks 'the empirical essence of Judaism.' He writes: 'What is the mundane basis of Judaism? Practical needs; self-interest. What is the mundane cult of the Jews? Huckstering. What is the Jews' mundane god? Money.' Marx denounces the Jews as prototypes of the commercial spirit and of a monetary economy; he makes Judaism the symbol of bloodsucking capitalism. The reader cannot escape the feeling that he is ostentatiously showing his opposition to Judaism, is demonstratively severing himself from his own race, and by emphasizing his anti-capitalist tendencies is declaring himself before all the world not to be a Jew. But one who takes so much trouble to declare that he is not a Jew must have reason for being afraid of being regarded as a Jew. I think there can be no doubt that this social factor of Marx's Jewish origin intensified his sense of inferiority, and must have increased his urge towards compensatory achievements."

And the anti-Semites never remind you that Karl Marx's bosom friend, sponsor, and cofounder with him of communism, was not a Jew but the German Gentile Friedrich Engels.

All of which means that Dr. Gartenhaus deserves to be heard.

But Dr. Gartenhaus doesn't spare unbelieving Jews. He denounces the Rabbis who claim that the New Testament is mostly propaganda designed to ingratiate the Christian Jews with the Roman authorities. He replies to them in detail. His chapter. "Modern Arguments Against Christ," is a detailed reply to the arguments of unbelieving Jews against Christ and Christianity. It is devastating.

And following that chapter, is the chapter on Jewish liberals and their fellow-travelers among professing Christians.

Dr. Gartenhaus, with apologies to neither Jew nor Gentile, sticks to the Christ of Bible prophecy, the Christ of the New Testament, the Christ of history.

At one point in Dr. Gartenhaus' argument I would not state the case exactly as he states it. In brief, he says that since the life and death of Christ were according to the plan of God, neither Jews nor Gentiles were ultimately responsible for the rejection and crucifixion.

I do not believe the Bible teaches that foreordination excludes individual and collective responsibility and guilt. The truth, it seems to me, is to be found in such passages as these:

"Surely the wrath of man shall praise thee: the remainder of wrath shalt thou restrain" (Psalm 76:10).

"The lot is cast into the lap, but the whole disposing thereof is of the Lord" (Proverbs 16:33).

"And we know that all things work together for good to them that love God, to them who are the called according to his purpose" (Romans 8:28).

But we all concede the profound mystery here. And in the context of Dr. Gartenhaus' stimulating book, he seems to be saying no more than that we should leave the issue where the Four Gospels leave it.

Those who know Dr. Gartenhaus—and I have known him for more than forty years—know that he has paid a heavy price for his faith in, and witness to, his Messiah. And that once he put his hands to Messiah's plow, he never looked back. For decades he has borne his witness, private and public, to his Messiah in all parts of the world. This book, one of the best of all his books, reveals that Dr. Gartenhaus' intellect is still keen and energetic, that his heart is still warm, that his sympathies are still cosmopolitan, that his courage is still lean and unbending.

He is a remarkable man with extraordinary qualities.

NOEL SMITH

Editorial Office
Baptist Bible Tribune
Springfield, Missouri 65801

Preface

Christ's Death:
Who Is to Blame?

This question has been settled forever and really should not be discussed further: "Therefore doth my Father love me, because I lay down my life, that I might take it again. No man taketh it from me, but I lay it down of myself. I have power to lay it down, and I have power to take it again. This commandment have I received of my Father." (John 10:17, 18). Again, "Then He said unto them, O fools, and slow of heart to believe all that the prophets have spoken! Ought not Christ to have suffered these things, and to enter into his glory? And beginning at Moses and all the prophets, he expounded unto them, in all the scriptures, the things concerning himself." (Luke 24:25–27). There are many, many other passages proving that Christ died to fulfill all scripture, according to the will of the Father.

The plain Bible teachings on this subject have been blatantly ignored by Christians down through the ages and have been perverted to "legalize" persecution against the Jew. The plain Bible teachings on this subject have been blatantly ignored and perverted by Jewish leaders down through the ages in their life and death struggle against anti-Semitic forces.

The many books, treatises and articles published on this subject generally fall into two categories: those which place all the responsibility for Christ's death on the Jews; and those which absolve the Jews altogether for that death—both categories obviously ignoring what God has to say about the matter. It is because men have chosen to ignore these plain Biblical truths that we feel impressed—yea, compelled—to write this book. This Satan-inspired accusation of "Christ-killers" continues to crop up with each new upsurge in anti-Semitic activity, both here and around the world; and many well-meaning but ignorant Christians are being swept up into this dangerous floodtide each year.

Writers on both sides—the accusers and the apologists—presumably have held the Satanic maxim that "the end justifies the means." In this frame of mind they both have fabricated "facts" and have converted idle legends into supposedly factual history. Both sides freely quote scripture pulled grotesquely out of context to prove a point, and both have been and still are disseminating falsehoods and half-truths which have led to confusion, hatred and malevolence —often resulting in outrageous criminal acts against each other.

All "Christ-killer" accusations are the direct result of "anti-Christs," leading ultimately to *the* anti-Christ mentioned in Daniel, Revelation and elsewhere. All such accusations are intended to leave Jesus in the grave and to shield the fact of his resurrection from the masses of people. Had Jesus' last name been Christ, and had He been but a man, a prophet, and a martyr, then some good conceivably could come from the insane debates over who killed Him; but, Christ is a *title*. It is the Greek rendering of the same Hebrew word rendered *Messiah*. If Christ had remained in the grave, there would be reason to debate who was, or is, responsible for His execution; but, Christ AROSE! "I am he that liveth, and was dead; and, behold, I am alive for evermore, Amen, and have the keys of hell and of death." (Revelation 1:18).

These plain Biblical facts notwithstanding, the question of who killed Christ—however variously stated—has been discussed from the time of the apostles until the present day. Historians, jurists, sociologists and Bible students have contributed to the promulgation and perpetuation of the libelous allegation that the Jewish nation is guilty of the death of Christ and therefore is a race so corrupt as to be deserving of contempt, if not outright annihilation.

Jewish victims of these falsifications used these self-same distortions to "prove" that the New Testament has corrupted and inhumanized the Goyim (Gentiles), causing hatred and persecution toward the Jews; therefore, Jewish leaders throughout the centuries have indoctrinated their people into believing that the New Testament not only is an anti-Semitic book, but also that it is the first and worst such book in all the world. They ignore the fact that anti-Semitism was born two thousand years before Christ, in Egypt. (For a fuller treatment of the subject, see the author's book *Anti-Semitism and Christianity*.)

Neither hate nor love looks for logic to explain itself. Logic, or even simple common sense, might have asked, "Just what sort of a god was it that poor mortals could murder him?" Or it even might have considered, "What possible difference does it make anyway—since He arose from the grave?" At the very least, logic would be expected to look into the "why" of the cross to see that God so ordained Jesus as the Lamb of God, that no other means could be provided for the redemption of fallen mankind, and that no power except that of God Himself could have intervened to prevent Christ's death. And, if that had happened, we still would be in our sins destined for hell.

It should be obvious to even the most casual observer that those leaders, scholars, clergy and lawyers who provided the masses with a pretext for hating the Jew did not derive their various charges *out* of the New Testament, but rather read them *into* it. Approaching the New Testament with bias, they sought to find confirmation of their antipathy and through casuistry, distortion and misleading interpretation, they brought forth "facts" concerning the wickedness of the Jews which culminated in the crucifixion.

Since the masses of Gentiles and Jews were illiterate throughout the dark Middle Ages—with no access to the New Testament—and had to believe what their leaders taught, they may justly be excused for their part in the violence and bloodshed prevalent during this historical period. But what possible excuse is one able to stand on in this, the 20th Century? The New Testament is freely available throughout the world—even in communist-controlled lands, though with some difficulty—and the Holy Spirit earnestly desires to lead us into all truth.

And the simple truth about the New Testament is that in letter and in spirit it disproves the anti-Semites' version of Christ's death and disproves Jewish charges that it is responsible for the woes that have befallen this people throughout the ages. Proof of these statements is presented in the following pages. The New Testament is a Jewish book—the most noted and most highly revered Jewish book in all the world—and it would be far more advantageous for this people to recognize the book as their own, to adopt it, defend it and promulgate it among all nations. Indeed, this precisely is what they will do during the great tribulation that is to come, and during the millennium following the tribulation.

CHRIST DIED FOR ALL

The death of Jesus Christ is not something about which to argue and quarrel. God decreed it for man's salvation: "For God so loved the world, that he gave his only begotten Son, that whosoever believeth in him should not perish but have everlasting life. For God sent not his Son into the world to condemn the world; but that the world through him might be saved." (John 3:16, 17). Had He not been put to death on the cross, He would not have become "Christ"—the "Lamb of God"—sacrificed for the redemption of the world.

Because God had so decreed, no power in heaven or earth could have prevented that death, that burial or that resurrection! There is no variableness, no shadow of turning with God. What was decreed before the foundation of the earth had to come to pass. Satan tried to prevent it when he tempted Christ in the wilderness and again when he used the voice of Peter to try and persuade Jesus against going up to Jerusalem. Satan tried to kill Jesus with grief in the garden, and under the load going up to Golgotha—anything to prevent His being raised up as was the brazen serpent by Moses. But God's infinite plan for the salvation of man was not to be discarded!

To argue who killed Christ, then, is theological nonsense—spiritual insanity, if you will. The death of Christ was not a tragic defeat, because it was followed by his glorious resurrection—by which He was made "Lord and Christ"—effectively installed in this exalted position, and thereby given "all authority in heaven and earth." (Acts 2:36 and Matthew 28:18).

NO SPECIAL GUILT CHARGED TO THE JEWS

It is most regrettable that some Christians condone their dislike of the Jews in the same manner as overt anti-Semites: by claiming that the Jews are cursed because they called for responsibility for Christ's blood to be on themselves and on their children in Matthew 27:25. But, this simply is recorded as an incident that occurred, and there is no suggestion from the Gospel story itself that this outcry reflects some divine intent of retribution. Indeed, the Gospels simply tell about the trial and crucifixion as it happened—setting forth the facts as the fulfillment of the Old Testament.

Neither Paul, nor Peter, nor any of the early Christians attribute any special retribution to the Jews for the death of Jesus Christ. One of the purposes of this book is to show that the ridiculous, senseless curse which the infuriated mob would have had inflicted upon themselves was of no effect.

Neither did the Jewish people *as a whole* reject Christ when He was among them—on the contrary, they loved and protected Him. If one were to blame all the Jews for the deeds committed against Jesus by some of their ancient rulers, then we ought to be honest enough to blame all the Gentiles for what the Romans did to Him—because the Romans were at that time rulers of practically all the "civilized" world.

The Jewish people at that time eagerly, longingly and prayerfully expected the Messiah to come and reestablish the Davidic kingdom, and for a time many hoped that Jesus was He—but there were several factors which caused doubt and disappointment, as we shall see further on in this book.

No, we cannot judge the ancient world by our standards. In the time of Jesus, the people did not have all the evidence available to us for accepting Him as the Savior of the world. Today, any intelligent person should easily become convinced that Jesus is what He claimed to be. His resurrection, His spiritual conquest over so much of the world, the tremendous impact which His teachings have had upon the lives of millions of people—all suffice to substantiate His claims that He was not a mere human being, that He possessed divine power and authority and that what He spoke was the Truth. These facts should be brought in love to the attention of modern Jews.

Immediately after Jesus was crucified as the lowest of common criminals, the great masses of people lost interest in Him: "Just another of those false pretenders to Messiahship," they thought. After His resurrection, however, when Peter showed them from their Holy Writ that He was predestined to suffer and die for man's salvation, thousands upon thousands believed on Him. Not many years after Christ's death and resurrection, multitudes of Jews in Judea and in the countries of the dispersion believed when it was proved to them that both the life and death of Jesus were in full accord with the predictions of the Holy Prophets. It was the Jews who first accepted Him and who disseminated the Gospel throughout the then-known world in the first and second centuries A.D.

Both Jew and Gentile may learn a lesson in love from Peter: at Pentecost, he directly charged the Jewish people to whom he was speaking with participation in the killing of Christ (Acts 2:23); on an occasion not long afterwards he pointed to the extenuating circumstances of their ignorance (Acts 3:17); and on both occasions he declared to them lovingly and compassionately that what was done was past and that it was God's will (Acts 2:23, 3:18). The question that arose concerned the future—that is, "What shall we do?"—and Peter answered, "Repent, and be baptized . . . for the remission of sins." (Acts 2:38). Notice that he did not require them to make certain amends such as paying a fine, doing certain penance or bringing a sacrifice to expiate for that sin. All he called upon them to do was to

"repent" and to "be baptized" in the Savior's name as an acknowl-
edgement of their repentance and faith in Him. Notice too that there
is no hatred, no malice, no pogrom initiated to punish this people.
There was a call to repent—not merely to repent for whatever share
they had in "killing" Christ, but repentance of sins in general. There
was no need for a new sacrifice because Christ already had offered up
the all-sufficient sacrifice for the sins of mankind. All that was—and
is—needed was for each sinner to claim that sacrifice for the remission
of his own sins (Acts 2:37, 38). Notice also that Peter addresses his
Jewish audience *after* the crucifixion with the words, "men and brethren" (Acts 2:39).

And we may learn a lesson from Paul. Though speaking of unbelieving Jews as those who "killed the Lord Jesus," he does not single out
this incident as accounting for their guilt. Rather, he includes their
treatment of God's messengers before and after the time of Christ:
"who killed . . . their own prophets, and have persecuted us; . . .
forbidding us to speak to the Gentiles that they might be saved, to fill
up their sins alway: for the wrath is come upon them to the uttermost."
(I Thessalonians 2:15, 16). Yet, Paul had the most passionate concern
for their salvation—"to the Jew first."

THE THESIS

In this book I hope to prove the following propositions, all of which
are contrary to current widely accepted notions:

1) The New Testament truthfully depicts the life, laws and cus-
    toms of the Jews in the time of Christ;
2) The Jewish people are no more guilty of the death of Christ
    than are the Gentiles;
3) The Jewish judges (Sanhedrin) followed proper legal proce-
    dure in the trial of Christ—moreover they had full authority
    to execute anyone whom they found guilty of a transgression
    entailing the penalty of death;
4) Christ committed acts which, according to the law as then
    expounded by Jewish teachers, entailed the death penalty
    —on their assumption that He was not what He claimed to
    be;
5) No human being could have averted the death of Christ, and
    we cannot explain how it could be that responsible creatures
    would play a role in this the greatest drama in history;

6) God has not rejected the Jews "because they rejected Christ," even though it is true that temporary "blindness in part" (Romans 11:25) has befallen the Jewish people; and

7) The Christian doctrines are not opposed to the Jewish religion, rather they are based upon it.

It is my sincere hope and prayer that this book will lead many to the truth and love which the New Testament teaches for both Jew and Gentile. It is my hope and prayer that both may be led to care more for what good one can do for others, rather than dwell on what wrong one has done to another in the past; and that both Jew and non-Jew may be led to care more for what Christ has done for man, rather than for what man has done to Christ. Instead of asking, "Who killed Christ?"—we should ask "What killed Christ?" The answer, of course, would be "OUR Sins."

Throughout this book, I have tried to put all bias from my heart in considering the question of Christ's death. I have tried to be true to the letter and spirit of the Bible "as it is written," not heeding any false assertions from either anti-Semites or philo-Semites—relying solely on God's Word as recorded in the Holy Scriptures.

May the Lord of love and mercy make this book a blessing to all— Jew and non-Jew alike.

Jacob Gartenhaus

Part I

Christ and the Jews: Then

Chapter 1

Jesus in the Eyes of
His Contemporaries

The Seed of Anti-Semitism

To introduce this chapter we will again refer the reader to the author's companion book, *Anti-Semitism and Christianity,* which treats the subject in detail. Generally speaking, anti-Semites fall into one of five main groups: Crude, Theological, Liberal, Communist and Jewish. These, in turn, can be sorted into three main types: hoodlums, cultured and religious, and it is with this more general classification that we will be dealing in this book.

The hoodlums always have been ready to kill anybody, Jew or non-Jew—just as long as they stand to gain something from their actions. They would rather kill Jews, however, because there is less danger of reprisal or retaliation—the Jews in exile usually have been defenseless. This group is incapable of reasoning or being reasoned to.

The cultured anti-Semites would not actually participate in atrocities themselves, yet overtly or covertly, directly or indirectly, they incite violence and assaults against the Jew. These, the refined, genteel anti-Semites sometimes are even more guilty than those who do the actual killing, maiming, raping, and so forth.

The religious anti-Semites—the "spiritualizers," the pietistic anti-Semites—are those with whom one should especially try to reason. They would not take part in any act that smacks of crime, nor would they incite others to such acts. They probably would dissuade people from hurting others, whether Jew or non-Jew. They would even shed some tears over atrocities—but, in the eyes of God, they are nonetheless guilty. Although they do not applaud the malefactors or approve of their actions, they acquiesce—or even find some justification for the killing. They reason: "It cannot be helped. It is an Act of God. They brought it upon themselves. They rejected Christ, and so God has rejected them. They are abandoned and accursed."

These religious anti-Semites are "killing" the Jewish people spiritually. By wresting a few words of scripture totally out of context, they teach that God is through with the Jewish people and that all promises which He gave them have been revoked and transferred to the Gentile church. Thus the Jewish people are kept from knowing the great blessings that could be theirs.

Not only is this an erroneous conception of God and His dealing with man—it is a dangerous heresy serving as an opiate to calm the conscience of the actual killer.

For the last 1900 years, the New Testament has been abused and misused by "Christian" anti-Semites to propagate hatred against the Jews. Horrendous crimes have been perpetrated against the Jews on the pretext: "the Jews rejected Christ and killed Him, therefore God rejected them and would have them to be persecuted in retribution." So-called "Christian" Jew-baiters have created a sort of vicious circle: because of their hatred they have misread and misinterpreted certain passages in the New Testament, and then, because of what they thought they found, they hate the Jews more.

Few of the luminaries of the Church have protested against these distortions. Not one, to our knowledge, has stated strongly enough that there is no hint in the New Testament that the Lord gave any human being the right to avenge Christ's blood; that not one word in the New Testament can justify any persecution whatsoever; and that all the so-called "anti-Semitic passages" are taken completely out of context. It is our hope that through the discussions presented in this volume Christians will find it worthwhile to reread the New Testament—prayerfully—disregarding old prejudices, lies and half-truths. Through this rereading, they will rediscover the plain, simple truth about the trial and death of Christ, and come to realize that the resurrection negated any and all discussion of "who killed Christ."

Some of the grossest distortions of history have been propagated by anti-Semites and have found credence and been adopted as truisms. Among these is the assertion that the men of the Sanhedrin were as a body corrupt, wicked and blood-thirsty creatures. To substantiate and reinforce these lies, Jew-baiters cite alleged violations of the law in the trial of Christ.

Anti-Semites often contrast the Jewish judges with Pilate, who four times examined Jesus and found Him innocent. The anti-Semites tend to see only the wickedness in the men of the Jewish tribunal, although technically they judged in accordance with the established law of the time, as we shall show later on. But Pilate is seen as the best in the history of jurisprudence. They fail to mention that Pilate violated every precept of justice by delivering Jesus, *whom he found innocent,* to his cruel soldiers to be scourged, mocked and then crucified.

The standard anti-Semite argument runs something on this order: The Old Testament rebukes the Jewish people again and again for their sins and crimes; they murdered their prophets as they later murdered Christ; the New Testament speaks of their evil deeds; Christ called them a "generation of vipers" in Matthew 12:34, and told them they were of their father the devil in John 8:44; and they have been known all over the world since their nascence as obstinate, quarrelsome, rebellious and sanguinary misanthropes; everywhere and always they have been hated, despised and persecuted; and in light of all this history to say that it is a result of Gentile perversity is utter nonsense.

Anyone well-versed in the Bible knows that God, when admonishing and chastising His people, has done so as a compassionate father disciplining and correcting his children. In spite of all their faults, God has called the people of Israel, "My people," "My firstborn," and other such endearing terms. After each condemnation there always followed compassionate consolation—for example, see Jeremiah 30:18-20. True, there have been Jews who killed the innocent and the righteous—there have been such people in all nations.

If we were allowed to follow the anti-Semites' example and cull Biblical passages out of context, we might conclude that all Gentiles are dogs, because Christ spoke of them as such in His conversation with the Syrian woman in Matthew 15:21-28 and Mark 7:24-30; yet no sensible Gentile accuses Christ of anti-Gentilism. And in His reference to a "generation of vipers" and "your father the devil," Jesus was not referring to all the Jewish people, but only to those who at that moment were trying to entrap and incriminate Him. These hecklers, Christ claimed, had no right to claim Abraham—the man of God—as their father. But for the Jewish people as a whole, Christ had only love, love which He confirmed with His lifeblood.

We all understand that He intended to teach the people around Him that where there is faith there is no difference between Jew and Gentile. He proved His love and compassion also for the Gentiles when He went over to their provinces, and healed their sick and fed their hungry—as in Matthew 15:29–39 and Mark 7:31—8:9.

God knew what He was doing when He elected this unworthy people to be His own. He knew what He was doing when He sent to them

His holy prophets and finally His only begotten Son, as we learn in Isaiah 43. And, "He hath not dealt so with any nation." (Psalm 147:20; cf. Deuteronomy 4:32–34 and Romans 3:1–4). The simple fact is, dear reader, that God cannot do anything wrong, cannot make any mistake, and cannot be taken by surprise by any man. How low and poor a concept of Almighty God we so often have! How wrongly we view Christ and His mission in coming to this wretched earth! How easily blinded to the Truth which is Christ!

John, whose Gospel so often is misquoted to justify anti-Semitism, reports Christ as saying, "Salvation is of the Jews." (John 4:22). Furthermore, this same John tells us that Christ "came unto His own" —meaning, of course, the Jews. Why God sent Him to His own, knowing that they would not receive Him, is a mystery, but one which Paul partly discloses in his epistles. Everything regarding His life, death and resurrection was predestined, as Christ said. All this transpired within the Jewish sphere, and only God the Father has the right to judge "His own."

Was Jesus Really Blameless?

To consider this question we need to look at the career of Jesus from the standpoint of a person living back then. Were the Jews really so wicked in persecuting and prosecuting Him? Was Jesus really so blameless in His life as a citizen of the Jewish State and as a member of society that no one had any right to molest Him? Should the established authorities have disregarded His extraordinary utterances, deeds and claims?

We know *NOW*, 1,900 years later, that Jesus was sinless. Before He had entered upon His ministry, John the Baptist proclaimed, "Behold the Lamb of God, which taketh away the sin of the world." (John 1:29). (See also Hebrews 7:26–27). *Now,* since that ministry has long ago run its course and has been followed by consequences which no mere human insight could have discerned; *now*—for us who stand this side of the cross and the empty tomb and the world-wide outreach of the Gospel—it is plain for all who have eyes to see that He was, and is, the sinless sacrifice for sin. Of this we know *now,* after all that was predicted about Him and affirmed by Himself has been fulfilled, except His second coming, which we pray will be fulfilled in the near future.

Now we know that as the Christ and the Son of God He had the right to do all that He did and to say all that He said.

But, the people in His time did not have the full body of evidence which is available to us. Even His own half-brothers did not believe at first. Even His faithful disciples were not altogether sure of His claims before He appeared to them after His resurrection, explaining to them, beginning with Moses and the prophets, that it had to be in this manner: "And he said unto them, These are the words which I spake unto you, while I was yet with you, that all things must be fulfilled, which were written in the law of Moses, and in the prophets, and in the psalms, concerning me. *Then opened he their understanding,* that they might understand the scriptures, And said unto them, Thus it is written, and thus it behoved Christ to suffer, and to rise from the dead the third day." (Luke 24:44–46. See also Luke 24:18–27; Mark 16:-10–14). *Before then* the people did not have such a perspective for viewing His person and work.

When some of the leaders asked Him for a sign to prove His claims, He referred them to the sign of Jonah (Matthew 12:38–40). And it was only after this sign was given that His disciples were fully established in their faith. Then, and only then, He became known to many of the people as the Messiah, and thousands of them believed in Him.

During His three years of ministry, Jesus—in the guise of man—said things and did things which, according to the prevalent laws, customs and practices were regarded as grave transgressions, and some of which were subject to the death penalty. Jesus, the incarnate, voluntarily subjected Himself to human behavior and functions, and to the laws of man and of nature—though, of course, the purpose of His mission required that at times He break these restraints.

We also have to take into account the conditions of His time. It was a very confused, precarious age. Any rash act by the people might have provoked the rage of the ever-watchful, keen-eyed Romans, who with their superior force could pounce upon the people, killing and destroying, leaving corpses and ruins.

The common people probably were ready to risk an uprising, since they figured they had little to lose in case of defeat. But the upper classes, the elite, the more learned, and especially the high priests who were appointed by Rome, knew only too well the catastrophic consequences for the people as a whole, and particularly for themselves. Thus they had valid reason to be alarmed over the activities of "that Galilean" who within three years succeeded in stirring up hopes of pristine glory, of freedom and independence.

They saw in Him an imposter, a revolutionary, a rabble-rouser, a trouble-maker: one who must be silenced before He inflamed the people to open rebellion. From their viewpoint, they had the grounds to arrest Him as a transgressor of the laws of the land. Jesus' acts and sayings were not clandestine. They were open and of common knowledge. Everybody knew that He broke some laws. Everybody knew His "disrespectful" attitude toward the leaders. Everybody knew that He claimed divine authority, a thing considered as idolatry.

So, there was sufficient reason to arrest this *man,* convict Him and put Him to death. We say, "this *man*" referring to the point that if Jesus was not what He claimed to be, as the Jewish leaders supposed, He was but a man and justly condemned.

A true answer to the question of His innocence or guilt is found in Isaiah 53: "It pleased the Lord to bruise him . . ."; "He was numbered with the transgressors . . ." And in I Peter 3:18: "For Christ also hath once suffered for sins, the just for the unjust, that he might bring us to God, being put to death in the flesh, but quickened by the Spirit."

Many of Jesus' acts and words tended to give offense to the law-abiding people, particularly the rulers and upper classes. His association with publicans and sinners (Matthew 9:10) gave offense, as did His fraternizing with the common people—the so-called Am-ha'ARETZ, the people of the land, the uneducated masses. And, while He showed so much love and compassion for the common people, His attitude toward the upper classes was that of disdain, disrespect and censure. His high regard and esteem for woman—who at that time was everywhere considered a second-rate creature—was held to be so revolutionary that even His close disciples marvelled.

Most important of all, however, is that in the eyes of the rulers some of His offences were punishable by death: blasphemy, the violation of the Sabbath laws, and seduction away from the faith.

In considering the question at hand, we should bear in mind that the most significant principles of Judaism throughout the centuries have been belief in Jehovah and observance of the Sabbath. And, it is to these two principles that most of the words of the Ten Commandments are devoted. The Lord Himself sanctified the Sabbath and rested on that day after the creation. This is the first commandment which He ordained. (Genesis 2:1–3). The Ten Commandments did not *first* institute observance of the Sabbath rest, and thus it is said: "*Remember* the sabbath day, to keep it holy." (Exodus 20:8) and "*Keep* the sabbath day to sanctify it, as the Lord thy God hath commanded thee." (Deuteronomy 5:12–15). The Sabbath rest was known to the Israelites previous to the giving of the law on Sinai. (Exodus 16:25, 26, 29–30).

The Pentateuch alludes to the law of the Sabbath several times, and the prophets protested infringements on these laws constantly. An example may be found in Leviticus 23 and Nehemiah 13:15–22. In Leviticus 23, the Sabbath leads the other holy days, and in the post-exilic period, its strict observance was regarded as a sign of national loyalty. The Maccabees even hesitated to violate the Sabbath when engaged in the defense of the country.

To desecrate the Sabbath was punishable by death (Exodus 31:-12–14; 35:2) and the first trial in Jewish history was of one who had desecrated the Sabbath (Numbers 15:32–35). In this instance, a man was found gathering sticks on that day and Moses, in doubt as to what punishment should be given for such disobedience, consulted God about the matter. The instruction was that the transgressor should be put to death. Even the gathering of the manna was forbidden on the Sabbath (Exodus 16:14–36).

During the Second Temple, divine services were celebrated on the Sabbath in synagogues, and Jesus preached at such services—as we learn in Matthew 12:9; Luke 4:16; John 6:59 and 18:20.

A certain Jewish sage said, "More than the Jews kept the Sabbath, the Sabbath kept the Jews."

The Jews were just as careful to keep the name of God holy as they were to keep the Sabbath holy. To desecrate His name was considered the most flagrant, odious sin imaginable. The smallest belittling remark about God or faith in Him was condemned as blasphemy—an offense requiring the death penalty.

Jesus, robed in humanity, was a citizen of the Hebrew state and thus subject to the prescribed laws regarding the Sabbath and God's name, and therefore liable to the required penalties.

Therefore, when the Pharisees drew His attention to the fact that His disciples were plucking ears of corn on the Sabbath—which in their eyes was a flagrant breach of the Sabbath laws—He justified the deed. (Matthew 12:1–8; Mark 2:23–28; and Luke 6:1–5). He Himself transgressed the Sabbath laws by healing the sick, where the illness was not so serious that the healing could not have been postponed for a weekday. (Matthew 12:10; Mark 3:1–5; Luke 6:6–11; and John 9:6–16). He even claimed to be the Lord of the Sabbath, with authority to do on that day as He pleased.

Like His attitude toward the Sabbath, His attitude toward God was considered highly blasphemous in the eyes of His contemporaries. His claims to divinity, divine authority, and divine power—indeed many of His utterances in relation to God—were regarded as stark blasphemy. So was His claim to be the Son of God and to have authority to execute judgment and forgive sins. (Matthew 9:2; John 3:16–18; and 5:25–27).

John often employs the word *"Jews"* instead of the "rulers" or the "antagonists of Jesus," in contrast to "the people," and "the common people," who loved Him and followed Him, and who, of course, also were Jews. These "common" Jews, "the people," were both despised and distrusted by the upper class, and it was because of them that no one ever dared stretch out a hand against Jesus—although there were several attempts made by the hirelings of the rulers as we see in Matthew 21:45, 46; Mark 11:18; 12:12; 14:1,2; Luke 19:47; 22:1–6; 22:53; and John 7:45–48 and 11:47.

Thus, in John 5:16–18 we read: "And therefore did the *Jews* persecute Jesus, and sought to slay Him, because he had done these things on the sabbath day. But Jesus answered them, My Father worketh hitherto, and I work. Therefore the *Jews* sought the more to kill him, because he not only had broken the sabbath, but also said that God was his Father, making himself equal with God." When Jesus asserted His deity to the people around Him, saying, "I and my Father are one" (John 10:30), their anger was so great that they were about to stone Him. After He succeeded in calming them, they exclaimed, "For a good work we stone thee not; but for blasphemy; and because that thou, being a man, makest thyself God." (John 10:33).

In the time of Moses there were two trials which ended in the sentence of death: the one mentioned earlier, and the trial of a man accused of blasphemy in Leviticus 24:11–16. In both cases, God was consulted as to the punishment, and in both cases He ordained that the transgressor be put to death.

A third deadly sin (Deuteronomy 13:6–11) which Jesus was guilty of under the laws of His time—as expounded by the teachers of the law—was that of seducing Jews away from their faith. In Matthew 14:33 we read: "Then they that were in the ship came and worshiped him, saying, of a truth thou art the Son of God." He did not protest and His acquiescence could be construed as leading the people away from God. This, of course, amounted to a violation of the second commandment, which forbade any worship besides that of God—upon the assumption that Jesus was not in fact the Son of God.

There were other "offences" committed by Jesus, which the people—especially the guardians of law and order—considered very grave, in light of their teachings and traditions.

For example, when His disciples were observed eating without having ritually washed their hands in accordance with Jewish custom, He was asked by the Scribes and Pharisees: "Why do thy disciples transgress the tradition of the elders? for they wash not their hands when they eat bread." (Matthew 15:2). Jesus' answer contained a statement which could only be regarded as highly outrageous to the Jewish mind: "Not that which goeth into the mouth defileth a man; but that which cometh out of the mouth, this defileth a man." (Matthew 15:11).

These words must have astonished even His disciples as they stood within hearing distance: "Then came his disciples, and said unto him, Knowest thou that the Pharisees were offended, after they heard this saying?" (Matthew 15:12). Jesus must have felt that they wanted an explanation, judging from the tone of their words, and in His explanation as given in Matthew 15:16–20, as if by one stroke of the pen, Jesus repudiated all the dietary laws which were then considered—and have ever since been considered—as the most important observance of practical Judaism. Even this pronouncement could be considered seduction away from the faith.

Another example is His attitude toward the Jewish divorce laws: "When a man hath taken a wife, and married her, and it come to pass that she find no favour in his eyes, because he hath found some uncleanness in her: then let him write her a bill of divorcement, and give it in her hand, and send her out of his house." (Deuteronomy 24:1). The rabbis, by the time of Jesus, had made it very easy for the husband to divorce a wife "who did not find favour in his eyes," but then came this man Jesus who made it so very, very difficult.

For instance, to the Jews Jesus would allow divorce only on the grounds of fornication (Matthew 5:31, 32), but for the Gentiles He would not allow it even on these grounds (Mark 10:11, 12).

What was most provoking was his oft-heard statement, "It hath been said . . . but I say unto you . . ." (Matthew 5:31, 32; and 19:-3–12).

Again, His pronouncement concerning the "woman taken in adultery" in John 8:3–11 must have seemed very strange to the legalistic Pharisees. According to the law of Moses (Leviticus 20:10 and Deuteronomy 22:22) such a woman should have been put to death —but according to Jesus there was not even the possibility of condemning her.

And, again, how strange and un-Jewish was the manner in which He spoke of His mother in Matthew 12:46–50, which could be considered a breach of the commandment which enjoins man to honor his mother.

Although most of the people revered Jesus, and although some even saw Him as a prophet, still they considered Him as but a man, and a Jew. As such, He was to observe the law of the land like all other Jews. But in their attachment to Him, they evidently were able to overlook His transgressions, and they always were ready to defend Him. The rulers, quite naturally, saw in all this a grave danger to established law and order—and accordingly, they decided that He should be liquidated. Were it not for the fear of the people, as mentioned, the rulers might well have caught Him sooner and convicted and executed Him. It was only on that Passover night, when all the people were asleep, that they could do away with him. (We know, of course, that all things happened according to God's Own time schedule.)

Thus we see that Jesus committed quite a long list of "trangressions" and that some of them were punishable by death, according to the laws of that time as interpreted by the Scribes and other rulers.

Had the rulers not been so afflicted with "blindness" (Romans 10:2) and if they truly had known the Torah—that is, as the spirit that enlivens and not as the letter that killeth (II Corinthians 3:6)—they surely would not have rejected Jesus as they did. For, He really did nothing contrary to the spirit of the Torah, acting in His role as the authentic expounder and administrator of its precepts. As He said, He "came to fulfill the Torah, not to destroy it." (Matthew 5:17).

The simple fact is that He could not have been guilty of blasphemy. When a Scribe asked which is the first commandment of all, Jesus replied, "To love God." (Mark 12:28–30). Whenever He spoke of God, it was only to honor and sanctify His name: He could not have blasphemed God, because He was God incarnate—but they did not know it.

Truthfully, He could not have been charged with the desecration of the Sabbath, according to the spirit, because He did nothing for His own benefit. What He did was in His capacity as Lord of the Sabbath and was only for the glorification of God. Furthermore, as He phrased it "the Sabbath was given for man, not man for the Sabbath," and He exemplified this statement by His actions.

Some false witnesses accused Him of desecrating the Holy Temple, but the rulers must have known how much He loved and honored the Temple. He often came there to preach and worship, and He even jeopardized His life by driving out the money changers in His zeal for its sanctity and purity.

He never uttered a word of censure or disrespect against the *proper use* of established authority, whether Roman or Jewish. As to the Romans, He said, "Render to Caesar the things that are Caesar's," (Mark 12:14–17), and as to the Jewish authorities, He exhorted the people to submit to those that "sit in the seat of Moses," (Matthew 23:1–3).

His criticism was directed entirely against the hypocrites among the rulers, the elders, Scribes, Pharisees and Sadducees, and against their abuse of their authority in society by domineering and suppressing the common people.

No, Christ did nothing against the spirit of the Torah.

As Paul termed it, if the rulers had not been so "blind" they would have discerned the Lord of Light and Glory, the Lord of the Sabbath, the Lord Who came to inaugurate the New Covenant of which Jeremiah had long before prophesied. (Jeremiah 31:26–36). They would have seen that the Old Testament was the preparation for the New, a teacher leading to Christ: ". . . Wherefore the law was our schoolmaster to bring us unto Christ, that we might be justified by faith." (Galatians 3:17–24). They would have known that Christ, the Messiah, had come to "redeem Israel from the curse of the law."

Had they known, they would not have crucified Him: "Which none of the princes of this world knew: for had they known it, they would not have crucified the Lord of Glory." (I Corinthians 2:8). "And now brethren, I know that through ignorance ye did it, as did also your rulers. But those things, which God before had shewed by the mouth of all his prophets, that Christ should suffer, he hath so fulfilled." (Acts 3:17, 18). "For they that dwell at Jerusalem, and their rulers, because they knew him not, nor yet the voices of the prophets which are read every sabbath day, they fulfilled them in condemning him." (Acts 13:27).

Again, why it was not given to them to see Jesus in His full effulgence, is a mystery which one might to some extent understand when prayerfully studying the Epistle to the Romans—especially Chapter 11 and verse 25: "For I would not, brethren, that ye should be ignorant of this mystery, lest ye should be wise in your own conceits; that blindness in part is happened to Israel, until the fulness of the Gentiles be come in."

To say that they were blind is not to exonerate them—not by any means. They did not see because they closed their eyes against the light. And while they did not have the measure of light that we now have, they did have light, and therefore, they were responsible for their rejection of Jesus Christ. The fact that they had less light then we—while not exonerating them—does provide what we may call an extenuating circumstance. They were right in that *if* Jesus was not what

He claimed to be, then He was a blasphemer and worthy of death. But if they had had no sin, Jesus would not have prayed for their forgiveness.

Using Jesus' Own example, let him who is without sin first cast a stone at those judges of Jesus—but we who are purified by the blood of Christ will say with our Master, "Father, forgive them; for they know not what they do." (Luke 23:34).

Chapter 2

Did the Jews Reject Christ?

This question and its companion about God rejecting the Jews have been the root cause of much of the anti-Semitism and anti-Semitic acts down through the previous 19½ centuries. It is past time for Christians to wake up to some simple, truthful answers to this and related questions. It is long past time for all Christians—especially non-Jewish Christians—to get back to the Bible "with a pure heart fervently," wherein one may find irrefutable answers to the anti-Semitic forces.

Did the Jews reject Christ? As a people, NO! Some *individual* Jews, yes. Let's turn this question around and consider just how silly and nonsensical it really is in the first place: Did the Gentiles accept Him? As a people, NO, but individual Gentiles did—but do we claim that the Gentiles as a whole thus have rejected Him and therefore God has rejected the Gentiles? Dares any man to claim that the Gentiles *as a whole* are Christian? By *Christian* we of course mean blood-washed, born again believers in Jesus Christ as crucified, buried and resurrected—that is, as the Lamb of God. This *Biblical* definition in one fell swoop eliminates a majority of those claiming to be "Christian" in the world today. The simple fact is that more Gentiles have rejected Him than have accepted Him. There are more Gentiles following Buddhism, Hinduism, Communism, Catholicism and other pagan cults than there are among the ranks of true Christianity. Wherein, then, is the logic of asking whether or not the Jews *as a whole* rejected Him?

But, with the Jews of the time of Christ, the opposite is the case more accepted Him than rejected Him—at least insofar as the specific events anti-Semites want to use as examples of "Jewish rejection" are concerned, as we shall see in the following discussions.

The Jews who did reject Him mostly were of the upper strata, the political and ecclesiastical leaders who were offended for certain selfish reasons—out of legalistic adherence to their understanding of the letter of the law—or because they saw Jesus as a hazard to the peace of the nation, as Caiaphas believed. These were few in number when compared to the multitudes—literally thousands—who paid homage to Him, who loved and adored Him, and who were ready at all times to protect Him from His enemies. The people *as a whole* were sympathetic with Him and His teachings. Many were in a sense "followers," or "disciples" of His regardless of how short they may have measured His full stature.

The common people often became perplexed—not knowing whether to side with Him or with the established authority—and we may well understand their dilemma as to whether or not He was the expected One. After all, His nearest friends, relatives and disciples had their doubts: "And John calling unto him two of his disciples sent them to Jesus, saying, Art thou he that should come? or look we for another?" (Luke 7:19). Nevertheless, no matter how many were skeptical, no matter how many sometimes wavered, we may categorically state that only a comparatively small number of the common people positively rejected Him.

And, one must bear in mind another important fact—that is that the early preachers and missionaries all were Jews. These were so successful in launching the Christian enterprise that within a relatively short period of time—less than 100 years—most of the then-known civilized world, which was the vast Roman Empire, had embraced Christianity. This great historical marvel cannot be explained as simply the results realized from the efforts of Paul, Peter, James, John, and the few Christian personalities known to us from the New Testament and other early literature. Nor can it be accounted for by including all of the 120 gathered together in the upper room. It must be acknowledged as the results gained from the efforts of the thousands upon thousands of Jews who had accepted Jesus as their Messiah before the destruction of Jerusalem who became zealous missionaries in the Diaspora. These went out not only to other Jews but also to the Gentiles among whom they lived. It was Jews of the Christian persuasion who mainly accounted for the rapid growth of the early church—a feat unequaled in any other period of church history.

In fact, early Christianity was so "Jewish" in nature that even among the apostles a controversy arose as to whether Gentiles should be admitted into the bond of Christian grace if they had not previously entered into the Covenant of Abraham by circumcision and observance of the rigorous laws and customs of Judaism. Paul's letter to the

Galatians gives insight to the extreme seriousness of this controversy.

It required an Apostle Paul, an authority in the Law as a Pharisee and an Hebrew of the Hebrews, to persuade the early Christians that there is no need for circumcision and the observance of the Law in order to be a child of God: "Wherefore the law was our schoolmaster to bring us unto Christ, that we might be justified by faith. But after faith is come, we are no longer under a schoolmaster. For ye are all the children of God by faith in Christ Jesus. For as many of you as have been baptized into Christ have put on Christ. There is neither Jew nor Greek, there is neither bond nor free, there is neither male nor female: for ye are all one in Christ Jesus. And if ye be Christ's, then are ye Abraham's seed, and heirs according to the promise." (Galatians 3:-24–29).

There was not the slightest doubt among the early church that the Jews had some priority in the Kingdom. The Jewish Christians were the stem of the tree upon which the Gentile Christians were grafted.

These Jewish Christians attended the synagogues for divine services together with the non-believing Jews for many years after the resurrection of Christ. The Christian movement generally was considered as a Jewish belief, although somewhat peculiar, and it was only after certain conflicts developed between these two factions that the Christians were forced out of the synagogues. But even after this separation the Jewish Christians seem to have lived in peace for many years with the other Jewish sects: "Then had the churches rest throughout all Judaea and Galilee and Samaria, and were edified; and walking in the fear of the Lord, and in the comfort of the Holy Ghost, were multiplied." (Acts 9:31).

Space does not permit the quoting of the many New Testament passages which show the intimate attachment of the people to Jesus. The Bible abounds with such references even from the beginning of His ministry: "there followed him great multitudes of people from Galilee, and from Decapolis, and from Jerusalem, and from Judaea, and from beyond Jordan." (Matthew 4:25). It was to these multitudes that He preached the "Sermon on the Mount" as recorded in chapters 5 through 7 in Matthew. Nor was it any different during the closing days of His ministry: the multitudes still were with Him, following Him, and adoring Him—and it was during these days that the miraculous feeding of 5,000 men (they didn't count the women and children present) was accomplished and on another occasion the feeding of 4,000 men. All of these followers—the recipients of His miraculous gifts—were Jews, with the exception of some Gentiles at the second "feeding." Zacchaeus could not get near Him for the press of the crowd—and many, many more instances could be called to mind where the multitudes crowded around Him. The greatest part, by far, of these multitudes were Jews—the common people.

In light of the preceeding discussion we see that the Jewish people did not reject Christ—if they had, the book of the Acts would not be in the Bible. But, we know that a certain faction of the Jewish people did in fact reject Christ altogether, and the Word is very clear as to who is included in this sadly self-deceived crowd: "The Son of man must suffer many things, and be rejected of the elders and chief priests and scribes, and be slain, and be raised the third day." (Luke 9:22). Note carefully what Jesus is saying here—it was the elders, the chief priests and the scribes who rejected Him; and not the common people.

Following the miracle of Lazarus' resurrection, the Pharisees were all the more aware of Jesus' marvelous influence on the people. This event and prospect so frightened them that, with the chief priests, they convoked the Sanhedrin for consultation. Caiaphas intimidated the Council by bullying and haranguing them and by telling how serious a catastrophe might result from allowing Jesus to do as He pleased. It was decided to eliminate Him: "Then gathered the chief priests and the Pharisees a council, and said, What do we? for this man doeth many miracles. If we let him thus alone, all men will believe on him: and the Romans shall come and take away both our place and nation. And one of them, named Caiaphas, being high priest that same year, said unto them, Ye know nothing at all, Nor consider that it is expedient for us, that one man should die for the people, and that the whole nation perish not. And this spake he not of himself: but being high priest that year, he prophesied that Jesus should die for that nation; And not for that nation only, but that also he should gather together in one the children of God scattered abroad. Then from that day forth they took counsel together for to put him to death." (John 11:47–53).

As for Lazarus: "Many people of the Jews, therefore, knew that he was there; and they came, not for Jesus' sake only but that they might see Lazarus also, whom he had raised from the dead. But the chief priests consulted that they might put Lazarus also to death, because, by reason of him, many of the Jews went away, and believed on Jesus." (John 12:9–11).

Thus a command was issued: "Now both the chief priests and the Pharisees had given a commandment, that, if any man knew where He were, he should shew it, that they might take Him." (John 11:57).

As an example of how the people "betrayed" Him in response to this command from the chief priests, Jerusalem had never before, nor has it since, witnessed a greater, more royal and spontaneous reception than that accorded to Jesus by the Jewish people just before the last Passover: "A very great multitude spread their garments in the way; others cut down branches from the trees, and strawed them in the way. And the multitudes that went before, and that followed, cried, saying Hosanna to the son of David: Blessed is he that cometh in the name of the Lord; Hosanna in the highest. And when he was come into Jerusalem, all the city was moved, saying, Who is this? And the multitude said, This is Jesus the prophet of Nazareth of Galilee." (Matthew 21:8–11).

The leaders were then convinced that the whole "world"—that is, people—had gone after Him and that nothing openly could be done to stop Him: "The Pharisees therefore said among themselves, Perceive ye how ye prevail nothing? behold, the world is gone after him." (John 12:19). It was only surreptitiously—in the dead of night when the "world" lay asleep—that the leaders could seize Him.

Although the people were asleep at the time, the leaders still feared that what was about to occur might reach the ears of some who would rush to the rescue of their beloved teacher. Therefore these cowards sent a large company of Roman soldiers and hirelings of the priests—together with Judas—to arrest Him. Of course all this was unnecessary, because Jesus stepped out to meet them and stated that He was the One whom they sought: "Jesus therefore, knowing all things that should come upon him, went forth, and said unto them, Whom seek ye? They answered him, Jesus of Nazareth. Jesus saith unto them, I am he. And Judas also, which betrayed him, stood with them. As soon then as he had said unto them, I am he, they went backward, and fell to the ground. Then asked he them again, Whom seek ye? And they said, Jesus of Nazareth. Jesus answered, I have told you that I am he: if therefore ye seek me, let these go their way." (John 18:4–8). Jesus knew their apprehension when He asked them: "Are ye come out as against a thief with swords and staves for to take me? I sat daily with you teaching in the temple, and ye laid no hold on me." (Matthew 26:55).

Even after the judges found Him guilty, for fear of the people they dared not execute the sentence of death. While they had convicted Him of a religious offense for which they themselves could put Him to death, they accused Him before Pilate as a political offender against the Roman rule to get Him under Roman jurisdiction. This, they hoped, would absolve them in the eyes of the people from responsibility for the death of their favorite leader.

Their fear of the people is told in several passages, for instance: "And consulted that they might take Jesus by subtlety, and kill him. But they said, Not on the feast day, lest there be an uproar among the people." (Matthew 26:4,5).

Again: "And they sought to lay hold on him, but feared the people; for they knew that he had spoken the parable against them; and they left him, and went their way." (Mark 12:12).

And: "And the chief priests and the scribes the same hour sought to lay hands on him, but they feared the people . . . and they watched him, and sent forth spies, who should feign themselves righteous men, that they might take hold of his words, that so they might deliver him unto the power and authority of the governor . . . and they could not take hold of his words before the people; and they marvelled at his answer, and held their peace." (Luke 20:19–28 in part).

Thus He unjustly was convicted as a rebel according to Roman law, and the priests succeeded in averting the wrath of the people from themselves. In a later chapter we will show that the Jewish court did in fact have power to inflict the death penalty.

Chapter 3

Did the Jews
Crucify Christ?

While this question is closely akin to the one regarding who killed Christ, still one can admit that, according to the Bible no man killed Christ because this power was in His hands alone, and yet in the next breath accuse the Jews—intimating the Jews as a whole—of rejecting and crucifying their Messiah. And, even though we readily see the inconsistency in the above reasoning, we are compelled to answer the accusation by virtue of its tremendous impact in all areas of Christendom. We already have seen that neither did the Jews as a people reject Him nor did the Gentiles as a people accept Him. We have seen that it was the elders, chief priests and scribes—the hierarchy and bureaucrats—who rejected Him and not the common people. Now, to answer the question heading this chapter, we will overlap somewhat into this same theme—that is, the love that the Jews, the common people, had for Jesus.

In Mark 12:37 we learn that ". . . the common people heard him gladly," and Mark also tells us how the people were amazed at His teaching: "And they went into Capernaum; and straightway on the sabbath day he entered into the synagogue, and taught. And they were astonished at his doctrine: for he taught them as one that had authority, and not as the scribes. And the scribes and chief priests heard it, and sought how they might destroy him: for they feared him, because all the people were astonished at his doctrine." (Mark 1:21, 22).

Luke tells us how all the people rejoiced at His deeds: "And when he had said these things, all his adversaries were ashamed: and all the people rejoiced for all the glorious things that were done by him." (Luke 13:17).

And in John we read: "Now when he was in Jerusalem at the passover, in the feast day, many believed in his name, when they saw the miracles which he did." (John 2:23).

"And many of the people believed on him, and said, when Christ cometh, will he do more miracles than these which this man hath done?" (John 7:31).

"Then said Jesus unto them, When ye have lifted up the Son of man, then shall ye know that I am he, and that I do nothing of myself; but as my Father hath taught me, I speak these things. And he that sent me is with me; the Father hath not left me alone; for I do always those things that please him. As he spake these words many believed on him . . . If ye continue in my word, then are ye my disciples indeed; and ye shall know the truth, and the truth shall make you free." (John 8:28, 29, 31, 32). "And many believed on him there." (John 10:42).

"Then many of the Jews which came to Mary, and had seen the things which Jesus did, believed on him. But some of them went their ways to the Pharisees, and told them what things Jesus had done. Then gathered the chief priests and the Pharisees a council, and said, What do we? for this man doeth many miracles. If we let him thus alone, all men will believe on him: and the Romans shall come and take away both our place and nation." (John 11:45–48).

We saw in Chapter 1 that during Jesus' lifetime the people vacillated in their faith in Him due to their very inadequate understanding of Him and His mission. After His resurrection, however, thousands upon thousands of Jews who heard the Gospel turned to Him with heart, mind and soul. Thus we have the testimony of the apostles: "Then they that gladly received his word were baptized: and the same day there were added unto them about three thousand souls." (Acts 2:41). "Howbeit many of them which heard the word believed; and the number of the men was about five thousand." (Acts 4:4). "And believers were the more added to the Lord, multitudes both of men and women." (Acts 5:14). "And it came to pass in Iconium, that they went both together into the synagogue of the Jews, and so spake, that a great multitude both of the Jews and also of the Greeks believed." (Acts 14:1). "These were more noble than those in Thessalonica, in that they received the word with all readiness of mind, and searched the scriptures daily, whether those things were so. Therefore many of them believed: also of honourable women which were Greeks, and of men, not a few." (Acts 17:11,12). "And when they heard it, they glorified the Lord, and said unto him, Thou seest, brother, how many thousands of Jews there are which believe; and they are all zealous of the law." (Acts 21:20).

It was these thousands of Jews—the "common people"—who either directly or indirectly bore witness to the salvation which comes only through Christ. They faithfully bore this testimony to all the nations where they sojourned both before the dispersion and especially afterwards.

The rulers never did like this people—that is, the "common" people: "Then answered them the Pharisees, Are ye also deceived? Have any of the rulers or of the Pharisees believed on him? But this people who knoweth not the law are cursed." (John 7:47–49). The upper classes—and especially the learned Pharisees—despised and hated the "common people," the so-called Am-ha'ARETZ which means those "who do not know the law," the uneducated. This class, of course, included women and children since women were not supposed to learn the law—and by some even forbidden to do so—and the male children had not yet learned it.

But Jesus seemed to have a special love for these, the "poor in spirit": "Blessed are the poor in spirit; for theirs is the kingdom of heaven. Blessed are they that mourn; for they shall be comforted. Blessed are the meek; for they shall inherit the earth. Blessed are they who do hunger and thirst after righteousness; for they shall be filled." (Matthew 5:3–6). He also loved the children: "But when Jesus saw it, he was much displeased, and said unto them, Suffer the little children to come unto me, and forbid them not; for of such is the kingdom of God." (Mark 10:14, see also Matthew 19:14 and Luke 18:16). He respected the women. He did not reject even those who were considered as outcasts, as were the publicans: "And when the scribes and Pharisees saw him eat with publicans and sinners, they said unto his disciples, How is it that he eateth and drinketh with tax collectors and sinners? When Jesus heard it, he saith unto them, They that are well have no need of the physician, but they that are sick. I came not to call the righteous, but sinners to repentance." (Mark 2:16,17).

Also, Jesus healed the "common" sick, fed the "common" hungry and heartily participated in the joys of the "common" people. He instilled in them a sense of self-esteem and convinced them that they were not worse than those of so-called higher society. He showed them that in the eyes of God they were no more unworthy than those higher up socially. He loved them and they loved Him: "But when he saw the multitudes, he was moved with compassion on them, because they were faint, and were scattered abroad, as sheep having no shepherd." (Matthew 9:36). "And Jesus went forth, and saw a great multitude, and was moved with compassion toward them, and he healed their sick." (Matthew 14:14). "And Jesus, moved with compassion, put forth his hand, and touched him, and saith unto him, I will; be thou clean." (Mark 1:41).

Among those who gathered around Him there were occasionally

those who thought that His words were incompatible with what was considered proper and hallowed by tradition. The resulting—and inevitable—disputes caused some to leave Him and some even to consider handing Him over to His adversaries, who sought His life. There even were those who went so far as to pick up stones with which to stone Him—but that is as far as they went, for no one ever laid hands on him. However, the greater number of the people, the "common" people—who always were gathered around Him and who loved and adored Him—would not permit any harm to befall their beloved Shepherd.

The opportunity for which the leaders were scheming came on that fateful Passover eve. All things were ready, and the hour was come for the scriptures to be fulfilled.

Emotions had run high throughout the previous days. Jesus had been acclaimed King by the multitudes. It looked as though things might come to a most dangerous climax on the Feast Day—a day when Jerusalem would swarm with pilgrims on the one hand, and with Roman soldiers and cohorts on the other hand ready to suppress any disorder or semblance of rebellion. The leaders and rulers could wait no longer (John 11:48), but realized that Jesus must be seized in the dead of night while the "common" people slept. Neither could there be an extended trial—all things must be brought to completion before the people found out what was being done.

So, Jesus was rushed through the proceedings and accused of blasphemy: "But Jesus held his peace. And the high priest answered and said unto him, I adjure thee by the living God, that thou tell us whether thou be the Christ, the Son of God. Jesus saith unto him, Thou hast said; nevertheless, I say unto you, Hereafter shall ye see the Son of man sitting on the right hand of power, and coming in the clouds of heaven. Then the high priest tore his clothes, saying, He hath spoken blasphemy! What further need have we of witnesses? Behold, now ye have heard his blasphemy. What think ye? They answered and said, He is guilty of death." (Matthew 26:63–66; see also Luke 22:66–71, Mark 14:61–64 and John 18:19–38).

Following His own confession He was sentenced to death. But, since the rulers still feared the vengeance of the people they delivered Him to Pilate. Their reasoning was simple—Pilate would judge Him according to Roman law as a traitor and insurrectionist, which also carried a sentence of death. They knew that by thus catching the "common" people unawares, the latter would not dare rise up against the overwhelming might of the Romans.

Their calculations proved to be correct—there hardly was any reaction to the death of Jesus. Most of them probably thought as did Cleopas (Luke 24:18–21), and reasoned that whereas He died—indeed, that mere human beings could kill Him—must be proof that He did not come in the name of God and thus was a false Messiah and just another imposter. They sadly acquiesced and turned each to his own affairs.

Did the Jews crucify Christ? No. After the rulers had taken Him to Pilate, all the things that happened to Him were at the hands of the Roman soldiers: "Then the soldiers, when they had crucified Jesus, took his garments, and made four parts . . ." (John 19:23 and see also Matthew 27:27 ff; Mark 15:16–25; and Luke 23:26–32). It was not the Jews, but the Roman (Gentile) soldiers obeying the orders of a Roman governor, Pilate, who nailed Jesus to the cross. Crucifixion actually was a Roman method of execution—the Jews probably would have stoned Him, according to tradition and custom—and this execution was of a man whom Pilate immediately before had declared to be innocent.

Yes, the Jewish high court had convicted Him of blasphemy and had sentenced Him to death—all within their legal powers under Roman rule. But He was executed by Roman soldiers, on order of a Roman governor, according to Roman law regarding insurrection, however farfetched—and this independent of the death sentence imposed by the Jewish court.

Not that it makes any difference anyway—the resurrection on the third day negated all this. Questions relating to human responsibility are considered in a later chapter.

Now, one may ask: "Who were those at the place of judgment before Pilate who cried, 'Crucify Him!' and took responsibility for His blood on themselves and on all the people of all succeeding generations?"

First of all, as we have mentioned, the meaningless curse that they would have brought upon themselves in Matthew 27:25 was just that—a meaningless statement. It never is mentioned again by the Lord Jesus, after the resurrection, nor is it mentioned by any of the apostles writing under the inspiration of the Holy Spirit.

Secondly, the great majority of the Jewish people at the time were a distance of many days' journey—even many months' journey—from the city of Jerusalem. The inhabitants of Jerusalem as well as the pilgrims who came there to celebrate the Feast of Passover at the Temple—in conformity with obedience of the Law—most probably were asleep during the trial of Jesus and the hasty procedure culminating in His crucifixion.

It was the night after a day of so very many activities—more so than at any other time in the year. This Holy night originated in the first Passover night in Egypt and it was a night fraught with profound mystery and symbolism: "And this day shall be unto you for a memorial; and ye shall keep it a feast by an ordinance for ever . . . It is a night to be much observed unto the Lord for bringing them out from the land of Egypt: this is that night of the Lord to be observed of all the children of Israel in their generations." (Exodus 12:14,42). The Hebrew words which are translated in the King James Version as "a night to be much observed" literally mean "a night of watching."

This night had its sublime finale with the Last Supper when Jesus Himself became the true Paschal Lamb: "Purge out therefore the old leaven, that ye may be a new lump, as ye are unleavened. For even Christ, our Passover, is sacrificed for us." (I Corinthians 5:7; and see also Matthew 26:19; Mark 14:12; Luke 22:7 and John 13).

Thousands of pilgrims and tourists filled the city and in addition to the preparations for the rites and ceremonies concerning the Paschal Lamb, it was the busiest day for businesses such as restaurants and inns. The evening following the sacrifice was the most solemn evening in Jewish life. The consumption of the sacrificial meal was accompanied by various symbolic ceremonies, recitations and prayers that lasted until late in the night—and some until early the next morning. After such a strenuous day and solemn night it may be assumed that most of the participants soon fell into a sound sleep.

We know from the Gospels that even the disciples could not keep awake even though they were enjoined by their Master to watch with Him: "And he cometh, and findeth them sleeping, and saith unto Peter, Simon, sleepest thou? Couldest not thou watch one hour? Watch ye and pray, lest ye enter into temptation. The spirit truly is ready, but the flesh is weak. And again he went away, and prayed and spake the same words, and when he returned, he found them asleep again, (for their eyes were heavy) neither knew they what to answer him. And he cometh the third time, and saith unto them, Sleep on now, and take your rest: it is enough, the hour is come; behold, the Son of man is betrayed into the hands of sinners." (Mark 14:37–41; and see also Matthew 26:40 and Luke 22:45,46).

Who made up the crowd that demanded Christ's death?

It was a nondescript rabble, a promiscuous collection of various sorts of people among whom were the servants and officers of the priests and Sanhedrin, who were kept awake and sent there to see to it that their sentence was executed without any hindrance by anyone.

Most of the crowd, however, probably were tourists, idlers, curiosity seekers—many of whom probably could not find a place to sleep in the overcrowded city. Some even may have come out of a morbid desire to see some hangings, since executions were normal under Pilate's rule.

When the crowd arrived at the place of judgment, they heard of three kinds of prisoners: two ordinary criminals; one political offender; and one religious transgressor. When the rabble was given the privilege of choosing one prisoner to be liberated, they naturally did not choose one of the murderers. It was to be either the political or the religious offender. It was relatively easy for the henchmen of the priests to induce the bystanders into calling for the liberty of the rebel Barabbas. Many considered him as a hero who had risked his life in plotting the downfall of the foreign power—an ideal almost all the people cherished: "And there was one named Barabbas, which lay bound with them that had made insurrection with him, who had committed murder in the insurrection." (Mark 15:7; and see also Luke 23:18). As for that convict named Jesus of Nazareth, he obviously did not care at all about politics, or about who was oppressing the people. He even endorsed the Roman rule by justifying the paying of tribute to them!

We may rightly suppose that friends and co-insurgents of Barabbas had come there to save their friend, and that they joined with the priestly clique for this end even though the two groups had little or no common interests otherwise.

Whoever composed that crowd, it is certain that it was *NOT* the Jewish people.

Chapter 4

Was the Jewish Court Trial Illegal?

That the trial of Jesus before the high priest was legal in all respects is readily proved in the Scriptures, and the *alleged* violations of the Hebrew laws cited both by Jews and non-Jews have no basis either in fact or logic. These *alleged* violations and/or irregularities are cited as *known facts* by anti-Semites to show how corrupt and vindictive the Jewish judges were whose eagerness to eliminate Jesus was fired by hatred—hatred intense enough to cause them to violate their own laws of legal procedure.

On the other hand, these *alleged* violations and/or irregularities are cited by Jews to prove by these very irregularities that the story of the trial of Jesus as recorded in the New Testament is largely a figment of imagination, written by persons who were unfamiliar with Jewish laws and customs but fired with a hatred for Jews. This group states flatly that Jewish judges of the highest court of justice could not have ignored the sacred laws of Israel: thus, the story must be false.

Herein is where both groups have got the cart before the horse, so to speak. It is the allegations that are false and the story that is true. In other words, the alleged violations simply are not true and the trial and conviction were *legally* proper, given the assumptions which the high court made regarding the *man* Jesus.

However, before we consider specific alleged violations we should be familiar with the Torah—the Jewish law—and with how it was put into practice by the rabbis (or judges).

The Jewish Law—The Torah—consisted of two parts: the *Written Law* (TORAH SH'B'KTAV) which is the code of laws written down by Moses in the Pentateuch as given by God; and the *Oral Law* (TORAH SH'BAAL-PEH), which according to rabbinic tradition was received along with the Written Law at Sinai.

According to the rabbis the Written Law consisted of 613 commandments, of which 248 were affirmative—"do's"—and 365 were negative—"don'ts." The position of the traditional Oral Law, then, was that of supplementing and interpreting this Written Law. For instance, the Written Law prohibits all work on the Sabbath, but does not state what activities are considered as work. Therefore, the Oral Law—as codified by the rabbis—stated practically every human action which might be considered as work and consequently forbidden on the Sabbath.

There must have been a large number of precepts relating to marriage, festivals, food and other matters which needed to be regulated but which were not dealt with sufficiently in the Written Law. The Oral Law—or "Rabbinic Laws," as they later were known—was assumed to have derived authority from the Divine revelation at Sinai.

Some evidence for the existence of an Oral Law is found in Old Testament passages speaking of "work" not mentioned in the Pentateuch: "Thus saith the Lord, Take heed to yourselves, and bear no burden on the sabbath day, nor bring it in by the gates of Jerusalem;" (Jeremiah 17:21). "Also we made ordinances for us, to charge ourselves yearly with the third part of a shekel for the service of the house of our God." (Nehemiah 10:32). "In those days saw I in Judah some men treading wine presses on the sabbath, and bringing in sheaves and lading asses; and also wine, grapes, and figs, and all kinds of burdens, which they brought into Jerusalem on the sabbath day; and I testified against them in the day in which they sold victuals." (Nehemiah 13:15).

The Mishnah Pirke Avoth tells us how the Oral Law was handed on from the time of Sinai: "Moses received the Torah and handed it down to Joshua; Joshua to the Elders, and the Elders to the Prophets, and the Prophets handed it down to the 'Men of the Great Synagogue.'"

Then, the oral part was passed from generation to generation by the leading rabbis until the time of Rabbi Judah the Prince (135–219 A.D.) who systematically arranged all the laws known in his time. His compilation of the Oral Law has been known as the Mishnah, or "Repetition." Rabbi Judah the Prince found it necessary to put into writing all the oral teachings and enactments of the rabbis since Hillel—who lived in the time of Christ—to the year 219 A.D. because there was the danger of this tradition becoming lost or forgotten following the dispersion. Thus the prohibition against writing down any law not written by Moses no longer was followed.

The development of the Oral Law did not end with the Mishnah, and with changing economic, social and political conditions, it became necessary to add, extend and amend laws. These developments were continued by rabbinic authorities for about 300 years after the Mishnah was compiled. These later compilations, along with the Mishnah, are known as the Talmud, or "Study."

When used without a qualifying adjective, "Talmud" usually refers to the compilation made in Babylonia. This compilation contains the discussions on the Mishnah by rabbis who resided in Babylonia from 200 years before the destruction of Jerusalem by the Romans to 500 years afterward—roughly 130 B.C. to 570 A.D.

In addition to the Babylonian Talmud there is the Jerusalem Talmud, which mainly is concerned with the discussions on the Mishnah by rabbis residing in Palestine after the destruction of Jerusalem. This Talmud is not as extensive as the Babylonian version, nor is it considered as authoritative.

The Talmud contains nearly 3,000 pages and consists of the laws regulating to the life of the Jew in all his waking hours—"from the cradle to the grave." The Talmud deals with ceremonies, festivals, social conduct, food, clothing, education, civil and criminal law, and so forth, and many of the regulations are intertwined with legends, fairy tales and superstitious beliefs. Until recent years every detail of Jewish life was shaped by the Talmud.

The legal decisions—Halachah—contained within the Talmud, along with laws enacted by some later authorities, were arranged into authoritative codes—but simplified for the average Jew. This first was done by Moses Maimonides (1135–1204) and later by Joseph Caro (1488–1575). Known as the Shulchan Aruch—"Set Table"—this code was final. Henceforth the rabbis refrained from enacting new laws and nullifying old ones. Prior to this, no rabbi was bound by any ruling of another rabbi unless the second was known to be of greater learning and sanctity. Presentday rabbis must abide by the decrees of their predecessors and no one dares to claim superiority over the "eagles" of the past.

Anyone familiar with the Pentateuch knows that God forbade the adding to or diminishing from His law—that is, the written law or "Law of Moses": "Ye shall not add unto the word which I command you, neither shall ye diminish ought from it, that ye may keep the commandments of the Lord your God which I command you." (Deut. 4:2).

At no time did the rabbis ever claim to "add to" or "diminish ought" from the law—they thought only to "interpret" God's laws by amendments and pronouncements. But by this "interpreting" procedure, some of the Scriptural laws were mutilated beyond recognition and if Moses were to see what now is known as "Judaism" he surely would not find very much resemblance to his Law. Yet, the rabbis always treated their enactments as though commanded by God Himself.

Regarding the question concerning the legality—rather the *alleged illegality*—of the Jewish court trial of Jesus, one should remember that all attempts to "prove" its *illegality* are based upon *rabbinic law,* and this itself presumed to have been in force in the first century in substantially the same form known to us from the much later writings. This position *ignores* two extremely important opinions on the trial: that of the *Bible,* generally; and that of *Jesus,* particularly—and these two opinions have One Author, that is, the Holy Spirit.

It should be mentioned at this point that during the period of the Second Temple there existed two major sects—the Pharisees and the Sadducees. The Sadducees often were very influential in both the government and the Sanhedrin and they contested the authority of the Pharisees to interpret the Law of Moses. The Sadducees judged more in strict conformity with the "letter" of the Law and if they were the judges at the trial of Jesus—which is possible—the laws enacted by the rabbis would have been disregarded altogether. In the latter event, of course, the basis for alleging violations of rabbinic law immediately would be dismissed.

The Jewish judges—as those to whom Christ referred as sitting in the "seat of Moses" in Matthew 23:2—possessed absolute authority to judge as they saw fit in each case. Disobedience to their judgment was a capital offense: "If there arise a matter too hard for thee in judgment, between blood and blood, between plea and plea, and between stroke and stroke, being matters of controversy within thy gates, then shalt thou arise, and get thee up into the place which the Lord thy God shall choose; And thou shalt come unto the priests, the Levites, and unto the judge who shall be in those days, and inquire, and they shall show thee the sentence of judgment. And thou shalt do according to the sentence, which they of that place which the Lord shall choose shall show thee, and thou shalt observe to do according to all that they inform thee, According to the sentence of the law which they shall teach thee, and according to the judgment which they shall tell thee, thou shalt do; thou shalt not decline from the sentence which they shall show thee, to the right hand, nor to the left. And the man who will do presumptuously, and will not harken unto the priests who standeth to minister there before the Lord thy God, or unto the judge, even that man shall die; and thou shalt put away the evil from Israel. And all the people shall hear, and fear, and do no more presumptuously." (Deuteronomy 17:8–13).

Their decision was as the decision of God—whether this decision was right or wrong, just or unjust. They even were called "Elohim"— Gods. Thus, in Exodus 21:6, where the English translation reads "Judges," the original Hebrew is "Elohim." See also Psalms 82:6 and John 10:34,35 for other examples.

The Jewish people were commanded to "make" judges in all their *gates:* "Judges and officers shalt thou make thee in all thy gates, which the Lord thy God giveth thee, throughout thy tribes, and they shall judge the people with just judgment." (Deuteronomy 16:18). As we shall see later, this location—that is, "gates"—is a very important point ignored by those who charge the judges of Christ with violating Hebrew laws.

The first judge in Israel was Moses, who was ordained by God. Soon it became evident that Moses could not handle this monumental task alone, and following the advice of his father-in-law, he appointed other judges to help him (Exodus 18:14-26). Moses retained authority to judge in all the hard cases and before he died he bestowed this supreme authority on Joshua—by "laying his hands upon him"—as ordered by God in Numbers 27:15–23 and Deuteronomy 34:9. Now, according to the Mishnah Joshua handed the Torah—and thus the authority to judge—to the Elders, who passed it to the Prophets, who in turn handed it down to the "Men of the Great Synagogue."

Various changes occurred in the political, economic and religious life of the Jewish people in the times of the Second Temple. Among other things, these changes gave birth to the Sanhedrin, which is known as the "Council" in the New Testament. This body assumed the supreme authority "to judge," although we do not know exactly when or how this was brought to pass. In addition, they gained the authority for the "laying on of hands"—that is, to ordain, to bestow the right to judge on any man they saw fit for the office.

During the period of the Second Temple, and for many years after its destruction, such ordination was performed by certain ceremonial rites. Later in the Diaspora ordination fell into disuse and was replaced by "examinations." By this latter method, a candidate for ordination would prepare himself through study and have himself examined by a rabbi of great learning. If the candidate was found qualified, he would be given the title of "rabbi" by the examining rabbi. Today, rabbinic degrees usually are conferred by rabbinical seminaries or Yeshivoth (Talmudic Colleges).

Modern rabbis generally exercise very little authority and are the subordinates of their congregations, rather than their masters and shepherds. But it was not always so, and we get an idea of the high esteem in which the people held the judges in the first century—and especially the High Priest, who usually was the Chief Justice—from the New Testament. John 11:51 speaks of Caiaphas in his High Priestly capacity as possessing the gift of prophecy even though he was not a very just man in his private life. Paul, in Acts 23:5, excuses himself for not knowing that the man who mistreated him, and of whom he spoke disrespectfully, was the High Priest.

In short, the judges of Christ were considered as "The Law"—their decision was final and not to be questioned. Thus, when we speak *today* of irregularities in *that* trial, we really are talking in terms that simply and strictly do not apply to the then-existing situation. To *allege* technical impropriety itself *constitutes* a technical impropriety because of the authoritative decision of that court. In other words, whatever one might claim to be an irregularity—with whatever show of logic—nevertheless would have to be classified as *not* an irregularity since the court sanctioned it.

That, dear reader, whether you like it or not, is simply the facts of the case. Regardless of this consideration, if we approach the trial of Jesus from the standpoint of how we might think the procedure did or did not logically correspond with what the laws of that time allowed or prohibited, we immediately encounter a formidable obstacle for those who wish to represent this trial as illegal and/or irregular. That obstacle is the difficulty of understanding just how any body of law —ancient or modern—is to be applied when we have only the bare precepts abstracted from the relevant judicial context. The layman might easily understand a statement in the statute book quite differently than would the lawyer; and even various lawyers might well disagree with each other over the same statement. We see this daily in our civil and criminal courts with the full body of law readily available for their research. Present-day *scholars* have but a few bare fragments to work with and therefore can hardly have even a fair *lay* knowledge of the legal situation obtaining in the first century. We simply are not in a position to say that the trial of Jesus was not in accord with the legal practices of that time.

Even if we grant for argument's sake that the modern scholars' interpretation of these laws is correct in every detail, there remain two further difficulties. The first is the lack of evidence that the laws allegedly violated in the trial actually were in existence at the time of the trial. These laws, hardly any of which have sound Biblical basis, were codified hundreds of years after Christ. The second is that even if these laws all did exist at the time of Jesus' trial, that it still is not certain that these were the particular laws followed at that trial. Because, as we have seen, the judges at that trial may well have been Sadducees, who were opposed to many of the enactments of the Pharisees—it being from the Pharisees that the later rabbinic laws supposedly were derived.

Furthermore, *both* rabbinic and Biblical law allow for *exceptions* in the legal process in certain circumstances. According to rabbinic principle, the normal laws were not valid in the case of seduction: ". . . the reverse may be done with a seducer as the Scripture (Deuteronomy 13:9) reads 'You shall not have any pity.' " (Gemara on "Mishnah Sanhedrin," chapter 4, Mishnah1). As we saw in Chapter 1, according to the conceptions of that time Jesus was a seducer—He claimed divinity and allowed people to worship Him. Thus, it may well have been that procedure otherwise to be followed was not deemed necessary in His case.

Mosaic law authorized the judges to make legal decisions as they saw fit in a time of emergency—even if it was not in agreement with the written law—and they could decide whether any particular situation was to be regarded as an emergency.

We already have discussed the fact that the time of Jesus was a time of continuous changes. It was a time when the lives of the people were conditioned by the Roman eagle, which hovered over the land ready to pounce with its pitiless claws at the slightest sign of rebellion. Aiding and abetting the ruthless Roman rulers were the Edomean Herods and the priestly Sadducean sycophants who, in league with certain judges, often could use the law to their own advantage.

In those perilous times there was much bitterness and dissatisfaction in the hearts of the common people against the foreign usurper and oppressor—as well as against their own leaders who often were no less oppressive than the Romans. Things seemed on the verge of open rebellion and the leaders had to be constantly on the alert to squelch any manifestation of uprising against established authority—whether Jewish or Roman. Exigencies often required prompt action in suspension of laws designed for normal times.

Intimidated by the High Priest, the judges of Christ may have found that His case was of extreme circumstances and thereby permitted the trial to be expedited without regard for the normal procedures.

Having thus laid the groundwork, we look now to the specific alleged violations and/or irregularities:

Allegation 1: Jesus was arrested, tried and condemned at night; whereas rabbinic law decreed that "no legal business could be conducted after sunset."

Rebuttal: The Law of Moses does not forbid holding trial at night. On the contrary, it says "at all times": "And let them judge the people at all seasons . . ." (Deuteronomy 18:22).

Allegation 2: Caiaphas caused Jesus to incriminate Himself, and the conviction was based on His uncorroborated confession.

Rebuttal: This was not illegal according to the Old Testament, which gives two examples—in Joshua 7:19-26 and II Samuel 1:16—of conviction and execution upon uncorroborated confession.

Allegation 3: The law, so it is claimed, required a written indictment, and there was none in the case of Jesus.

Rebuttal: There is no such law mentioned in the Bible.

Allegation 4: The trial was begun and concluded in one day; supposedly a "flagrant" violation of the law.

Rebuttal: There is no such law mentioned in the Bible.

Allegation 5: It is claimed that the Hebrew law required captial offenses to be tried in the "Hall of Hewn Stone" within the Temple, whereas Jesus was tried in the parlors of the High Priest.

Rebuttal: There is no mention in the Law of Moses of any so-called "Hall of Hewn Stone." According to Moses, important cases were to be brought originally before the priests, and that is where Jesus was brought. Deuteronomy 16:18 commands that they make judges "in all thy gates," as discussed earlier in this chapter.

Allegation 6: The verdict of the Sanhedrin was unanimous for His death according to Mark 14:64. Supposedly, according to Hebrew law, if the vote of condemnation was unanimous, it was taken for granted that the judges had failed in their duty as defenders and so the accused had to be released immediately.

Rebuttal: There is no mention in the Law of Moses or anywhere else in the Bible of any such law.

Allegation 7: Because the testimony of the two witnesses against Jesus was false and not in agreement (Matthew 26:60), it is alleged that He should have been released at once and the false witnesses slain—Deuteronomy 19:18–21 is cited in this connection.

Rebuttal: In the case of Jesus, the testimony of these false witnesses was not a material factor. Jesus could not have been convicted on their charge, even if it had been true. What Jesus reportedly had said, according to these witnesses, would have been regarded as hardly more than idle boasting and, while sacreligious, certainly not entailing the death sentence.

Allegation 8: No trials or executions were to be conducted on a holiday; and, of course, Jesus was condemned and executed at the Passover.

Rebuttal: On the contrary, it was customary to postpone judgment of transgressors *until* a holiday, so as to provide for a more public exhibition—the better to impress the people. See Rashi on Deuteronomy 17:13 in this regard.

Allegation 9: The High Priest broke the law by rending his clothes upon hearing Jesus' "blasphemous" words.

Rebuttal: The same Talmudic tractate cited here as Hebrew law also says that after the judges had heard either the accused himself or one of the witnesses utter the words of blasphemy, "they were to arise and rend their garments." ("Sanhedrin," chapter 7, Mishnah 6).

It is most significant that the Gospels make no charges of any breach of contemporary law in that trial. The only mention of any wrong-doing on the part of anyone associated with the arrest, trial and execution are the words of censure against the over-zealous servant who smote Jesus. If this action was censured by Jesus, as small as it was, how much more would any illegalities or irregularities have been censured by the Living Word?

What we must say is that the whole trial was a tragic wrong—while as far as we know it was not technically improper—committed as a result of ignorance of Jesus' true identity. But we must remember that the trial was in accordance with "the determinate council and fore-knowledge" of God, and brought about that we might receive forgiveness of all our sin.

A more detailed discussion of some other aspects of this trial will be found in the following chapter.

Chapter 5

Were the Authors
of the New Testament
Ignorant of Judaism?

In Chapter 4 we saw that the trial of Jesus was legal in all respects and that the legality of it may easily be proved from the Scriptures. We considered this facet at some length. In this chapter we want to consider two modern claims that really are quite beside the point and which could well be ignored as far as the main line of our inquiry is concerned. However, they do illustrate how utterly irrelevant and untrue some of the anti-Christian arguments can be. For this reason, we treat them here rather than in the chapter devoted to the trial itself. It might be well for the reader to review the above chapter before diving into this one where we will be considering the claims that (1) the Jewish judges at that time could not have executed a sentence of death, and (2) death by crucifixion was used only by Romans and never by Jews.

In pursuit of this misleading polemic, critics of Christianity always cite passages from the Talmud, which was written several hundred years after Christ and whose authors certainly knew less of events in Palestine in the time of Christ than did the authors of the Gospels who lived in Palestine at the time or shortly afterwards. The laws and customs prevailing in the year 30 A.D. cannot be assumed to have been the same as those known only from sources of 200 to 500 years later. It is from these latter sources that all argument on the illegality of Jesus' trial is derived, while overlooking entirely what the Bible has to say about it.

In fact, the laws and customs that prevailed in Jesus' time were not the same as those enacted at a much later date. The Romans did not interfere in the religious laws and practices of the Jews. They left to Jewish courts the full authority to put to death any offender whom they found quilty of a capital crime, according to the laws of the land. The Jewish courts *did* execute persons whom they condemned to death —and there even were deaths by crucifixion pronounced by Jewish authorities. Verification of these facts will be presented later in this chapter.

Some rabbis explain that the authors of the Gospels must have known better than the stories they wrote, but gave their "erroneous" account because of hatred for the Jews. Other rabbis are more polite and say that it was a time when the Christians in the Roman Empire were persecuted as a secret Jewish sect. Thus they found it necessary to ingratiate themselves with the Romans by trying to make them believe that Jesus, their Master, was favored by the Roman ruler in Palestine, who in turn sought to save Him from the bloodthirsty and fanatical Jews.

The answer is obvious. If the authors of the New Testament were mere propagandists seeking to influence the Romans, or Gentiles at large, they certainly would not have reported how Jesus considered the Jews to be the children of God and non-Jews to be nothing but "dogs." (Mark 7:27). Nor would they have revealed that Peter, considered the greatest of Christians, denied his Master three times. It is doubtful that they would have mentioned that Jesus stated, "Salvation is of the Jews." (John 4:22). It is unthinkable that they would have exclaimed what a coward Pilate was to crucify a man whom he had just declared to be innocent. Nor would they have related how cruelly the "brave" Roman soldiers treated Christ; and Paul, the apostle to the Gentiles, certainly would not have praised the Jews so highly as he did in his Epistle to the Romans (chapters 9 and 11).

No, the New Testament obviously was not written to spread hatred of the Jews nor to misrepresent the facts to further the interest of the Christian movement. Never have authors written anything more objectively and more truthfully than have the authors of the Gospels. It is written just as it happened, without comment or expression of personal feeling.

As to the claim that the Jewish judges at that time could not have executed a sentence of death and that the power of life and death in the Roman provinces was the exclusive prerogative of imperial *legatus,* Jewish apologists turn to John 18:31 for support: "Then said Pilate unto them, Take ye him, and judge him according to your law. The Jews therefore said unto him, It is not lawful for us to put any man to death." They also cite a particular passage in the Talmud which states that forty years before the destruction of the Temple the right to try capital cases ceased in Israel. (Even if the latter assertion is true, the time corresponds approximately with the time of the crucifixion and thus a death sentence might well have been rendered in the case of Christ.)

Furthermore, certain portions of the Talmud are quoted to indicate that the procedure of a trial in a capital case was so lenient and so compassionate that a death sentence by a Jewish court was well nigh impossible. The apologists claim that even when the Jewish courts had the right to execute those whom they condemned to death, they were to do all within their power to release the accused. The Jewish people's aversion to capital punishment supposedly was so strong that a court which once in seven years pronounced the death penalty was branded as "murderous."

We have proof from the Mishnah, which is the original, older and most important part of the Talmud, that Jewish courts did try capital cases and did in fact execute death sentences, even during the forty year period alluded to above. According to Mishnah Sanhedrin 7:2, the Sanhedrin convicted the daughter of a priest for committing adultery, and she was put to death. This happened only a few years before the destruction of the Temple, and many other statements in Tannaitic literature (Mishnah) disprove the later Talmud's statement about court authority during this forty years.

But, something of much more importance is pointed out in the above passage from Mishnah Sanhedrin 7:2, and that is that already a few years after the destruction of Jerusalem, even the most important oral laws had been forgotten and had to be revived by relying upon the memory of some trustworthy eyewitness—if such could be found. In this passage is a discussion of how the punishment of "burning" was to be done. While it was generally considered that it should be done by thrusting a hot lead string through the mouth into the inwards and thus burn the entrails, Rabbi Eliezer ben Zadok—as an eyewitness—said, "Once a daughter of a priest, having sinned, was surrounded with fagots and burned." He was answered, "The court which so ruled was ignorant of the exact law." Rabbi Eliezer lived in the first century, before and after the destruction of the Temple, and was considered as one of the greatest authorities on Jewish law. The Sanhedrin founded many laws (Halachoth) on some of his reports and reminiscences.

The significance should be obvious. If, during the time of Christ, even some of the most important oral laws had been forgotten, how much weight can be given to a compilation of 200 to 500 years after the time of Christ as evidence of what could or could not have taken place in the trial of Christ? Not only that, but fact and fiction, legend and history are all mixed together in the Talmud and are completely unreliable as historical facts. For any scholar to teach that the trial of Jesus was illegal or irregular based on Talmudic references is ignorance of the highest level.

As to John 18:31, the accusers of Christ only demonstrated their pusillanimity and subservience. Why did they have to tell the Roman ruler what the Roman law was—especially after he told them that they should take Jesus and judge Him according to Jewish law? Pilate did not have to be reminded of what the Roman law was. It was not the policy of Rome to interfere with the religious laws and customs of those people she conquered.

The Sanhedrin, which lasted in Judea until the destruction of the Temple, had full power and authority to condemn a Jew for transgressing the religious law, even to the extent of inflicting capital punishment. Josephus tells us that Titus—at the siege of Jerusalem—appealed to the Jews to surrender and reminded them that the Romans never interfered in the religious life of the Jews, even when they executed a Roman citizen for passing beyond the barriers of the sanctuary. (Josephus: Jewish Wars 6:2, 4; also 5:5, 2). In this case we are reminded that according to Jewish law, no foreigner was permitted to enter the Temple Court. Slabs were placed in front of the Temple with inscriptions in Greek and Latin prohibiting a non-Jew from entering, on pain of death. This law, and its penalty, were respected by the Roman authorities.

Philo (*Delegations to Gaius,* 38) and Josephus (*Jewish Wars* 2:11, 6) both testify that the Roman procurators generally abstained from all interference with the laws and customs of the country. In addition to civil laws, there are only two cases in which the Romans disregarded the Jewish religious law—once when Pontius Pilate brought his Roman legion into Jerusalem with the figures of the emperor on their shields, which was a breach of the Jewish law against idolatry, and again when Emperor Gaius Caligula ordered his statue erected in the Temple. Rome was especially lenient with Judea because she had learned to respect the religious scruples of Judaism—and not only in Palestine, but also throughout the empire as well. Among the other religious dispensations to the Jews of the empire was the right of the Sanhedrin both to try and to execute religious offenders.

For example, the Jewish judges did not hesitate to convict Stephen, nor did they hesitate in stoning him to death. They did not relegate this right to the Romans. (Acts 6:8–17 and 7:57–59). Josephus also tells of a Sanhedrin, convened by the high priest Ananus, which condemned and executed James, the half-brother of Jesus, for transgressing the law. (Josephus, *Antiquities* 20:9; see also Acts 12:1, 2). Obviously this is contrary to the words of the judges to Pilate—that it was not lawful for them to put a man to death.

Concerning the alleged aversion to capital punishment on the part of the Jewish judges, we may refer once again to Josephus. There we may read of the convictions by the Sanhedrin convened from time to time by Herod the Great. Herod's own wife, his own children, and many, many others were "legally" put to death. We read in the Talmud of one great judge and president of the Sanhedrin, Simeon ben Shetach—brother of the Hasmonean Queen Alexandra (Salome)—who upon one occasion sentenced and executed eighty women at Ashkelon who had been convicted of sorcery. Not only that, but he also condemned and executed his own son after relatives of those women took revenge by bearing witness against his son—accusing him of a crime which involved capital punishment. (Yer. Sanh. 23b).

Thus it is abundantly clear that not only were the Jewish courts free to try capital offenses and execute judgments, but also they actually put to death people so condemned. Crucifixion also was practiced by the Jews as a form of death penalty. (See Josephus: *Antiquities Book XIII*, Chapter XIV/2). Here the historian tells of an incident where the Hasmonean king, Alexander Sanneaus, crucified eight hundred opponents. (See also, *Jewish Wars* 4:6).

Referring to the mode of execution is entirely misleading, because the New Testament does not say that the Jews nailed Jesus to the cross. It quite plainly reports that His crucifixion was at the hands of Roman soldiers on orders from the Roman governor. This aspect was discussed at length in Chapter 4.

In other words, it matters not a bit whether the Jews did or did not practice crucifixion when discussing the death of Christ. It readily is admitted that the Jews did not crucify Christ, and this admission is based upon clear testimony of the New Testament.

According to some Jewish historians, there were at the time of Christ two Sanhedrins in Judea: one political and one religious. This theory first was advanced by Adolf Buchler in 1902 and has since gained an increasing number of adherents. The religious Sanhedrin supposedly was composed primarily of Pharisees and concerned with religious matters and the relation of the State to foreign countries. Only the religious Sanhedrin, it is said, was guided by statutes or established laws. On the other hand, the political Sanhedrin was appointed by the head of State, and it may be presumed that such men were appointed as would render decisions in accord with the ruler's wishes. This Sanhedrin was not guided by statutes, and could convene for cases at any place and at any time—day or night, weekdays or holy days—at the behest of the ruler. Jesus, according to these sources, was tried before just such a court convened by Caiaphas.

This pretty little theory of two Sanhedrins is a new invention—probably for apologetic reasons—but the Talmud makes no mention of two different groups in its large tractate dealing with the Sanhedrin. Nor did the later codifiers know anything about them; nor did Josephus; nor did the "ignorant" authors of the Gospels. But, even if this theory was correct, the position we maintain as to the technical propriety of Jesus' trial would not be affected. Indeed, if Jesus was tried before the type of Sanhedrin which the theory assumes, then all claims of "irregularities" would necessarily—and logically—be negated. And of course, this theory would in no wise affect the accuracy of what the Gospels report.

In view of the evidence cited thus far, it would be more effective for those seeking to discredit the New Testament's reliability to take a completely different approach and say that, since the Jewish court did in fact have the authority to inflict the death penalty, John 18:31 must be in error. Some Christian scholars seek to defend John's Gospel on this point by arguing that the Roman policy changed from time to time—that is, the Jewish judges were permitted to execute offenders during some periods but not during Pilate's administration. This apologetic is much on the same line as the theory of the two Sanhedrins—and while possible, is very doubtful, and very unnecessary.

We are able to see the trial of Jesus in its true light only by assuming that His Jewish judges did have the authority and power and right to inflict the death penalty. The correct interpretation, by making the Gospel narrative more readily understandable, does much to establish its reliability.

Approached from this standpoint, John's narrative shows that at first Pilate did not know what charge the Jews were bringing against Jesus, except that He was some kind of wrong-doer, or criminal. When Pilate asked, "What accusation bring ye against this man?", they answered, "If he were not a malefactor, we would not have delivered him up to thee." (John 18:29–30). Whereupon Pilate said to them, "Take ye him, and judge him according to your law." When the Jewish judges replied, "It is not lawful for us to put any man to death," they evidently meant that such was not to be done *in those particular circumstances.* Their contention was that Jesus claimed to the a "king" and therefore to be regarded as an insurrectionist against Rome—thus properly a subject only for the Roman tribunal. Cases which concerned their own law, exclusively, could be handled by the Jewish judges up to and including executing the death penalty—as evidenced earlier in this chapter. But here, in the case of Jesus, they were representing the matter as involving *more* than Jewish law. Thus, since the nation of Israel was subject to Rome, Jesus' case—involving violation of Jewish and Roman law—must be referred to the jurisdiction of the higher tribunal.

This interpretation fits what follows perfectly. Pilate proceeded to ask Jesus, "Art thou the King of the Jews?" (John 18:33), having been informed by "others"—the Jewish accusers—that Jesus had made such a claim (verse 34). Jesus answered, "My kingdom is not of this world," (verse 36), and He went on to say in effect that His was the kingdom of "truth" (verse 37). Pilate must have understood that Jesus' supposed "kingdom"—which no doubt seemed altogether visionary and idealistic—was not of such a nature as to compete with the mundane interests of Rome. Therefore Pilate declared to the Jews, "I find in him no fault." (John 18:38).

However, the Jewish leaders persisted, and at length were successful in exploiting the political implications, as well as personal implications for Pilate, in Jesus' claim to kingship. We should not overlook one very significant incident in the midst of all this: at one point, Pilate told the Jews in exasperation, "Take ye him, and crucify him: for I find no fault in him." (John 19:6). This seems to indicate that the Jewish judges did have power to put one to death. If it be argued that they had such power here only because Pilate had just given it to them, this question must be faced: "Why, then, did not the Jews go ahead and crucify Jesus themselves? Why did they go on demanding that Pilate sentence Jesus to execution?"

Whether we say they did or did not inherently possess the power of capital punishment, this much is clear: the Jewish leaders wanted Pilate to do it so that responsibility for Jesus' death would be placed on the Romans. It is conceivable that Pilate, had he pronounced a sentence of *guilt* on Jesus, would have granted the Jews the right to execute this sentence. But since he declared Jesus *innocent* on the charge on which his court was asked to adjudicate, it seems that in telling the Jews to "take Him and crucify Him," he was telling them to exercise their inherent prerogative of sentencing and executing an offender in accordance with the Jewish law.

Thus we may understand their response: "We have a law, and by our law he ought to die, because he made himself the Son of God." (John 19:7). They were saying that as a matter of fact there were proper Jewish grounds for consigning Him to death—but they were saying it to re-state in different terms that there also were proper Roman grounds. That Jesus was said to have "made himself the Son of God" had implications as to how far-reaching His pretensions of kingship were, and how serious a threat to the supremacy of Rome. This made Pilate "the more afraid" (verse 9) and he began to think that perhaps Jesus' claim might not be so inoffensive to Roman dominion after all.

The leaders finally prevailed. After Pilate purposed to release Jesus, they cried out: "If thou let this man go, thou art not Caesar's friend: whosoever maketh himself a king speaketh against Caesar!" (John 19:12). They then made their most decisive thrust when Pilate, still intent upon releasing Jesus, asked: "Shall I crucify your king?" The chief priests answered: "We have no king but Caesar!" (John 19:15). At this, Pilate yielded.

Chapter 6

Was Christ's Death
a Jewish Crime?

We have seen that no man took the life of Jesus; that the Jewish people did not reject Christ; that the Jews did not crucify Christ; that according to Old Testament—Biblical—Law, the trial of Jesus was not illegal or irregular in any respect; and we now turn to the question of responsibility—that is human responsibility in relation to divine purpose. Was Christ's death a Jewish crime? To what extent are the Jews responsible for His death? It seems absurd, in light of what we have seen in the preceding chapters, that this question would even be asked. Because of the number of Christians and anti-Semites who persist in pressing these inane prejudices and questions, we deem it important to provide a Biblical answer that is true to the Spirit of the Scripture.

Because they did not reject Jesus, the great majority of the people cannot be held responsible for His death. When Peter, in Acts 2:23 and 3:13–15, and Paul, in I Thessalonians 2:15, speak of the Jews as having put Christ to death, their words evidently are intended to apply only to those men who had some part in bringing about the crucifixion, or who at least consented to it. As for those Jews who were in some way involved, Jesus said unto Pilate, "He that delivered me unto thee hath the greater sin." (John 19:11). "They answered, and said unto him, If he were not a malefactor, we would not have delivered him up unto thee . . . Pilate answered, Am I a Jew? Thine own nation and the chief priests have delivered thee unto me. What hast thou done?" (John 18:30,35). We see, then, that it was the Jewish rulers who had thus "delivered" Jesus.

We already have noted the extenuating circumstances of these rulers' sin—that is, their ignorance of the full import of the deed. Still, sin it was—and greater sin than on the part of the Roman governor. But, here is a point almost everywhere overlooked by Christian and anti-Semite alike—no matter how great was the sin of the Roman governor, the Roman soldiers, the rabble-rousers who asked for Barabbas, the Jews who consented, or the elders and chief priests, Jesus' prayer on the cross was ". . . Father, forgive them; for they know not what they do." If this action was not laid to their charge by God the Father, God the Son or God the Holy Spirit, then by what insane reasoning can man charge them? The only sin they have to answer for is the one we have to answer for—that is, the rejection of Jesus as Savior. They were forgiven by Jesus, and therefore by all the Trinity, for being used as blind instruments in His death. Need we say it—if the Trinity forgave them, should not we forgive them?

There is no hatred for any people in the New Testament. There is only love and the invitation to salvation for all—and that "to the Jew first."

After all, the question of human responsibility in the death of Christ is quite secondary—if even that. What is most significant—and what the New Testament has by far the most to say about the death of Christ—concerns the divine purpose of providing our salvation. If one single fact stands out throughout the entire Bible—Old and New Testament alike—it is that God ordained Christ's death: "For God so loved the world, that he gave his only begotten Son, that whosoever believeth in him should not perish, but have everlasting life." (John 3:16). These words, the most sublime and holy ever written by human hand, expressing the quintessence of the Holy Scriptures, tell with unmistakable clarity the consummation of the Almighty's plan of salvation. We refer the reader to the books of Romans and Hebrews and Revelation as well.

Now come those who would make it seem that it was not God who gave His Son as an atoning sacrifice, out of love for fallen man, but that the Jews—by some supernatural power—snatched away His Son and murdered Him for their own selfish purposes.

We do not know what might have happened if the Jewish rulers had not rejected Jesus. If they had crowned Him as their expected King-Messiah, how would the Romans have reacted? How would Jesus have atoned for the sins of the world? How would He have conquered death? To finite, puny human minds, the life and death of Jesus—the sacrificial Lamb of God—are an inscrutable mystery. All that man can do—indeed, all that he is required to do—is to prayerfully and worshipfully accept it in reverential awe.

We do know that the Jewish role in the life and death of Jesus is a part of God's plan of salvation, in which Christ crucified and resurrected is the center and circumference. No creature has the right to ask God, "Why did it have to be so, and not otherwise?" It is a sin, a grave sin against the Holy Ghost, to pervert scripture as an excuse to damn and persecute the Jews. Christ's blood is not to be avenged —it is to be GLORIFIED! It is to be claimed by every man as the substitutionary sacrifice for the atonement of sins! It was for *no other reason* that Christ left the glories of heaven to take on humanity some 1900 years ago.

It is utterly astounding that faithful Christians and Bible scholars —in their hasty judgment of the Jews as "Christ-killers"—seem to forget the real Christ, His character and His task. From their words, one gets the picture of Christ as a helpless, defenseless and passive victim of the scheming Jews who sought His death. In their sick prejudice against the Jews, they seem to forget that Jesus was a voluntary victim and that He even was the High Priest who offered Himself up as a sacrifice for all mankind—both Jew and Gentile. They seem to forget that He was—and is—the Creator, Supporter and Preserver of all things (John 1:3 and Colossians 1:16,17) and that despite His death He could raise Himself back to life: "Jesus answered and said unto them, Destroy this temple (meaning His body) and in three days I will raise it up." (John 2:19). Again: "No man taketh it from me, but I lay it down of myself. This commandment have I received of my Father." (John 10:18).

The most significant fact is not that the Jewish rulers plotted His death, but that His death was "plotted," foreordained, long before any Jews were in existence. His Father planned His death and Jesus in obedience to His Father consented. Only Jesus Himself could have prevented His death—neither the Jews nor anybody else could affect this plan in any sense.

Jesus the Christ was not the victim of the Jews. Their role in that divine-human drama must be seen in light of the doctrine of election— the Jewish people had not so much chosen God as He had chosen them. We do not know why this is so. It is an unfathomable mystery, as Paul discusses in Romans 9. We do know that He did elect them to be His people and although He led them through hard tests and trials—and chastised them severely—it was out of love (Amos 3:2 and Deuteronomy 8).

God allowed Israel to be enslaved in Egypt for some 400 years. We do not know why. He brought them out when His time came. Again, we do not know why He held them in such favor. He sent His prophets to them—but, why to them only? He sent His only begotten Son to them, knowing beforehand that Jesus would be rejected by their rulers. Why has He chosen them to be the special instruments of His purpose? We have to confess that we do not know. We do know that He did so choose them and we are not to question the wisdom of His will. We are not to meddle with His eternal designs, which for some reason revolve in a special way around the Jewish people.

We can understand but little of the Jewish role in the death of Christ, but what we can understand is sufficient for our needs—that is, that His death was to provide salvation for man, "to the Jew first, and also to the Greek."

If those who say the Jewish people ought to be punished for their "crime" of "murdering" Christ would consider what the Word of God has to say about the subject—and would believe what the Word says— they certainly would be expected to change such an opinion. In the Word of God such people would find that ultimately it was God Who was responsible for the death of Jesus; that in a sense Jesus Himself is to "blame" for His own death; and that *no special guilt* is charged against the Jewish people. Nor, in fact, is any special guilt charged against the Roman governor and his soldiers. These two simple truths are so easily lost in the stream of hatred issuing forth from the human heart—and all such hatred is inspired of Satan. The true, born-again Christian certainly should not be found in this camp.

In any respect, those who would wreak vengeance upon the "guilty" for that "crime" certainly should not blame the presentday Jewish people—because only a very, very few would be even remotely kin to the rulers and those others who participated in some way in the trial and death of Jesus. And even those few participants, even as responsible creatures, were actors in a drama which they did not understand. Jesus Himself said that they did not know what they were doing and asked for (and received) their forgiveness. Certainly no man was given the right to "avenge His blood," as we have stated before.

Throughout His ministry Jesus was aware of the fact that He came to this world for the express purpose of laying down His life for the salvation of man. Before He yielded up His spirit on the cross He said, "It is finished!" (John 19:30). What was finished? "Jesus saith unto them, My meat is to do the will of him that sent me and to finish his work." (John 4:34). "I have glorified thee on the earth: I have finished the work which thou gavest me to do." (John 17:4). The book of Hebrews explains this in minute detail.

Why was all this necessary? It certainly is beyond man's comprehension. Perhaps this mystery will be revealed to us after the final defeat of the evil one and the Second Coming of Christ. In the meantime, it is enough to know that the Father, in love for the world, sacrificed His only begotten Son; and out of love that passeth all understanding, the Son voluntarily offered up His life for the world (John 10:17,18). "Even as the Son of man came not to be ministered unto, but to minister, and to give his life a ransom for many." (Matthew 20:28). "For Christ also hath once suffered for sins, the just for the unjust, that he might bring us to God, being put to death in the flesh, but quickened by the Spirit." (I Peter 3:18). ". . . Thus it is written, and thus it behooved Christ to suffer, and to rise from the dead the third day." (Luke 24:46). "For he hath made him to be sin for us, who knew no sin; that we might be made the righteousness of God in him." (II Corinthians 5:21). "Christ hath redeemed us from the curse of the law, being made a curse for us: for it is written, Cursed is every one that hangeth on a tree." (Galatians 3:13).

Perhaps, under the limitations to which He voluntarily submitted His human nature, during His last moments on the cross He still thought that God might spare His life when He cried out: "Eli, Eli, lama sabachthani? that is to say, My God, my God, why hast thou forsaken me?" (Matthew 27:46). But He saw that God's will must be done in this way and, "He yielded up the ghost." (Matthew 27:50). The original language for "yielded up the ghost" is literally "dismissed His spirit," implying an act of free will. This expression taken with Mark 15:37, "And Jesus cried with a loud voice, and gave up the ghost"; Luke 23:46, "And when Jesus had cried with a loud voice, he said, Father, into thy hands I commend my spirit, and, having said this, he gave up the ghost"; and John 19:30, "When Jesus, therefore, had received the vinegar, he said, It is finished! and he bowed his head and gave up the ghost," differentiates the death of Christ from any other physical death.

It had to be so—and not otherwise. Neither Satan, nor the impetuous Peter, nor Caiaphas and his underlings, nor Pilate and his cohorts, nor Jew-haters of all generations could have altered this the divine plan for the salvation of sinful man. "The Son of man must suffer many things, and be rejected of the elders and chief priests and scribes, and be slain, and be raised the third day." (Luke 9:22). "The Son of man must be delivered into the hands of sinful men, and be crucified, and the third day rise again." (Luke 24:7).

His most faithful followers did not understand why He had to die; they were dumbfounded and in despair. After His resurrection He first told it to the faithful women at His grave; then He explained it to those distressed doubters on the way to Emmaus, that it had to be so (Luke 24:25,26). Somewhat later He also explained it to His disciples (Luke 24:43–47).

He had to die even as a base criminal in order to accomplish what His Father planned for Him: "For I say unto you, that this that is written must yet be accomplished in me, And he was reckoned among the transgressors: for the things concerning me have an end." (Luke 22:37). When Peter wanted to rescue Him from His captors, Jesus said: "Thinkest thou that I cannot now pray to my Father, and he shall presently give me more than twelve legions of angels? But how then shall the scriptures be fulfilled, that thus it must be?" (Matthew 26:-53,54). John quotes Him, saying, ". . . the cup which my Father hath given me, shall I not drink it?" (John 18:11).

The apostles finally understood that it had to be thus because of "the determinate counsel and foreknowledge of God." (Acts 2:23; cf. 3:18; 13:25–29).

Hundreds of years before the birth of Christ, Isaiah already had revealed that most awesome plan of God to give His Son as a lamb for the vicarious atonement of fallen humanity.

There were several occasions when Jesus could have "backed out" of His decision to die as a sacrifice. For instance, at the beginning of His ministry, Satan tempted Him to give up His connections with God and so turn aside from that path leading up to the cross—but Jesus repelled his overtures. Later, when Jesus disclosed to His disciples that He soon was to suffer and die, Peter, His most trusted disciple, tried to dissuade Him from going to Jerusalem to His death. Jesus reproved Satan in Peter—because in this attempt to avert the death of Jesus, Peter was being used by Satan (Matthew 16:21–23).

If Jesus did not want to die for mankind He very easily could have stayed away from Jerusalem at the Passover festival. He knew beyond a shadow of a doubt what was in store for Him there: "And Jesus, going up to Jerusalem, took the twelve disciples apart along the way, and said unto them, Behold, we go up to Jerusalem; and the Son of man shall be betrayed unto the chief priests and unto the scribes, and they shall condemn him to death, And shall deliver him to the Gentiles to mock, and to scourge, and to crucify him. And the third day he shall rise again." (Matthew 20:17–19; see also Mark 10:32–34; Luke 18:31–34; Matthew 12:38–42; 16:21–28; and 17:22–23).

Jesus knew that Judas was about to betray Him—so He easily could have hidden somewhere until daybreak, when no one would dare lay hands on Him "for fear of the people." This fear of the people always had stopped His enemies when they wanted to hurt Him or to seize and deliver Him up to the judges.

Furthermore, at the trail He could have denied any serious charge brought against Him. He was not convicted by evidence brought against Him by others, but only by His own confession of what then was considered blasphemy. And later, before Pilate, He easily could have cleared Himself; but He did not deny His Kingship—although He averred that it was not of this world (John 18:37).

Even in the last moment of His life, He could have summoned angels to rescue Him—and at any time the mere spoken word from His lips could have destroyed this entire world which He spoke into existence (John 1:1-3). But He wanted to fulfill His Father's wish, which also was His own—for He and the Father are one. He had to lay down His life for "His sheep" to accomplish the work of redemption which was foreknown before the foundation of the world: "Who his own self bare our sins in his own body on the tree, that we, being dead to sins, should live unto righteousness: by whose stripes ye are healed." (I Peter 2:24).

Chapter 7

Has God Rejected the Jews?

For a detailed treatment of this question we refer the reader to the author's companion book, *Anti-Semitism and Christianity*, as this allegation is one of the first you hear from anti-Semites in their vociferous hatred for the Jewish people. Some theologians argue that, "yes, the Jews *were* the chosen people—but since they rejected Christ, God in turn has rejected them." We have, of course, seen that the Jewish people did not "reject" Christ and nowhere does the Bible intimate that God rejected His people for this or any other cause. The covenant He made with Abraham is an *everlasting* covenant, and if this "everlasting" covenant can be nullified, then none of Christendom can have assurance of "everlasting life." This is simple, basic Bible-centered logic since there is "no variableness nor shadow turning" with God or with Jesus who "is the same yesterday, and today and forever."

Following the resurrection when Jesus appeared to His disciples, He ordered them to carry His Gospel to all the world: "And said unto them, Thus it is written, and thus it behooved Christ to suffer, and to rise from the dead the third day; And that repentance and remission of sins should be preached in his name among all nations, beginning at Jerusalem." (Luke 24:46,47). "But ye shall receive power, after that the Holy Ghost is come upon you: and ye shall be witnesses unto me both in Jerusalem, and in all Judea, and in Samaria, and unto the uttermost part of the earth." (Acts 1:8).

He obviously knew nothing about His Father's so-called "rejection" of the Jews.

The disciples asked the risen Lord if the kingdom would at this time be restored to Israel. They had no doubt that it was to be restored— their only question was about the time of the restoration, and wondered if it was to be restored as a sequel to Christ's victory over death. Jesus answered, "It is not for you to know the time or the seasons, which the Father hath put in His own power." (Acts 1:7). Jesus' answer thus assumes that the restoration is to take place—but not immediately to their situation. Nor are they to know how far in the future this event is to occur.

Peter knew nothing of this supposed "rejection" of the Jews, and even when he severely admonished the Jews he called them "brothers" and, with a heart filled with love, urged them to repentance. Instead of suggesting any breach of the old covenants between God and His people, Peter proclaimed that God now was reaffirming those promises: "For the promise is unto you, and to your children, and to all that are afar off, even as many as the Lord our God shall call." (Acts 2:39).

Neither did Paul know anything of God's having "rejected the Jews." On the contrary, "to the Jew first" was the rule of his ministry. Concerning the Jew, he says: "my brethren, my kinsmen according to the flesh: who are Israelites; to whom pertaineth the adoption, and the glory, and the covenants, and the giving of the law, and the service of God, and the promises; whose are the fathers, and of whom as concerning the flesh Christ came, who is over all, God blessed for ever. Amen." (Romans 9:3–5).

If that were not sufficient to put down the "rejection" heresy, Paul emphatically states: "I say, then, Hath God cast away his people? God forbid. For I also am an Israelite, of the seed of Abraham, of the tribe of Benjamin. God hath not cast away his people whom he foreknew . . . I say, then, Have they stumbled that they should fall? God forbid; but rather through their fall salvation is come unto the Gentiles, to provoke them to jealousy. Now if the fall of them be the riches of the world, and the diminishing of them the riches of the Gentiles, how much more their fullness?" (Romans 11:1,2,11,12).

Centuries before the New Testament era, Zechariah prophesied of these bounteous "riches" which ultimately would come through the Jews to all nations: "And it shall come to pass, that as ye were a curse among the nations, O house of Judah, and house of Israel; so will I save you, and ye shall be a blessing: fear not, but let your hands be strong." (Zechariah 8:13). And, centuries before the time of Zechariah God already had promised to Abraham's seed: "and in thee shall all families of the earth be blessed." (Genesis 12:3).

Time and again the Jewish people have broken the covenant which God had made with them. Time and again God justifiably could have revoked His part of the covenant and destroyed them, but He always "remembered" His promise to Abraham and forgave them: "God is not a man, that he should lie; neither the son of man, that he should repent: hath he said, and shall he not do it? or hath he spoken and shall he not make it good?" (Numbers 23:19). "Then will I remember my covenant with Jacob, and also my covenant with Isaac, and also my covenant with Abraham will I remember; and I will remember the land." (Leviticus 26:42).

The most serious covenant violation perpetrated by the Jewish people occurred soon after the great event of revelation on Sinai—when God gave the Law in the hearing of all the people. Shortly thereafter, they went back on their promise to serve Jehovah alone and made themselves an idol—the golden calf—to be their god. God, then, would have been just in annulling His covenant and destroying them. As Moses pleaded with Him to forgive them, so Christ pleaded for them on the cross—even for the few who rejected Him. And, as God "repented"—that is, repented humanly speaking—"of the evil which He thought to do unto His people" (Exodus 32:10–14), there is every reason to believe that God forgave His people of their share in the death of Christ. Surely Christ's plea was at least as efficacious as that of Moses. No theological casuistry can counteract that plea coming from the Son of God.

Already too much has been written about the words, "Then answered all the people, and said, His blood be on us and on our children." (Matthew 27:25). It is clear that those who so clamored amounted to only a minute fraction of the Jewish people. We have seen that most of the people in Jerusalem would have been asleep at the time these words were spoken, and by far the majority of Jews were living outside Jerusalem and outside Palestine in the Diaspora. None of this vast majority had even the slightest knowledge of what was occurring that night. That rabble certainly had no authority to implicate all the people and their progeny for succeeding generations.

How can any man of common sense think that God became a partner to this infuriated mob by fulfilling their thoughtless wish?

Moreover, according to the New Covenant: "In those days they shall say no more, the fathers have eaten a sour grape, and the children's teeth are set on edge. But every one shall die for his own iniquity: every man that eateth the sour grape, his teeth shall be set on edge." (Jeremiah 31:29,30; see also Ezekiel 18). These words of self-condemnation for the blood of Jesus amount to a senseless, wicked demand, which God never granted.

Even if we could assume that God willed to punish these people and their children, we still must remember that even under the Old Covenant the iniquity of the fathers was visited on the children only until the third and fourth generation, and no longer (Exodus 20:5; cf. Exodus 34:7 and Deuteronomy 5:9).

We may assume further that after the bloody wars and the destruction of Jerusalem no remnant of these people and their children survived. But, even if we could assume that some did survive, who today can point to a Jew and say that he is of the fourth generation of that mob? Such a man would be at least 1,800 years old, and even if this were possible, where would one get the authority to punish such an one? Certainly not from any passage of Scripture.

They who have cited those words of imprecation in order to justify atrocities against the Jews have committed a grave sin. Not only have they sinned against the innocent victims of this *perverted* interpretation of the Word of God—they have sinned against God by representing Him as consenting to, or even encouraging, these atrocities.

Still there are some Christians who persist in propagating the old heresy that God changed His mind and cast the Jewish people aside. To substantiate this illogical heresy they usually quote Matthew 21:43: "Therefore say I unto you, The kingdom of God shall be taken from you, and given to a nation bringing forth the fruits thereof." This verse is pulled grotesquely out of its context to prove that the kingdom was taken from the Jews. The fact is that the whole chapter is devoted to showing how the Jewish people loved Jesus and how they revered Him as the "son of David."

To whom then was Jesus referring? Jesus very clearly, very plainly and very pointedly tells us to whom He was referring: "Jesus saith unto them, Did ye never read in the scriptures, The stone which the builders rejected, the same is become the head of the corner; this is the Lord's doing, and it is marvelous in our eyes? Therefore say I unto you, the kingdom of God shall be taken from you, and given to a nation bringing forth the fruits of it. And whosoever shall fall on this stone shall be broken, but on whomsoever it shall fall, it will grind him to powder. And when the chief priests and Pharisees had heard his parables, they perceived that he spoke of them. But when they sought to lay hands on him, they feared the multitude, because they regarded him as a prophet." (Matthew 21:42–46).

Is not the answer obvious enough for even the most simple to recognize? It was only the elders, the chief priests and the scribes who were against Him and these leaders in essence held the keys to the "Kingdom of Heaven" (Matthew 23:13) and it was from them that Jesus said the Kingdom would be taken and given to another people. Then Jesus goes on to tell us to whom it was given: "And I will give unto thee the keys of the kingdom of heaven: and whatsoever thou shalt bind on earth shall be bound in heaven: and whatsoever thou shalt loose on earth shall be loosed in heaven." (Matthew 16:19; cf. 18:18, 19). Here, of course, He was talking to the disciples who were to open the door of Christian opportunity to Israel on the Day of Pentecost and to the Gentiles at the house of Cornelius. The point is that the kingdom was taken from the chief priests, the scribes and the elders and given to the "people"—the common people whom Jesus loved and who loved Him.

It is absolutely certain from the context of the scriptures that Jesus did not mean to annul the Covenant, to revoke the Promises, or to deprive His beloved Israel of its destined glory. The multitude who at that moment stood around Him and whom the leaders feared, were His faithful adherents. In Matthew 21:43 the word "nation" obviously refers to "people" or "persons." Otherwise, to what "nation" was the kingdom given? If nation refers to "Church," as some people aver, it nevertheless is true that Christ's Church at first was composed altogether of Jews. And it was to these believing Jews that Jesus promised to give the same authority as had been exercised by the Jewish priests, elders and scribes.

But, even if we were to take these words to mean not just the leaders, we still have no warrant for speaking of a *final* "rejection" of the Jewish nation, because this passage has nothing to do with the immutable, irrevocable Covenant and the promises bound up therein. The New Covenant of Jeremiah 31 is between God and *His people,* "Israel"—not the Gentile "church" to the exclusion of Israel, as the allegorizers would have us to believe.

This people Israel are the same people whom He exiled from their land and whom He promised to bring back to their land—a promise which now is in process of fulfillment.

In saying that "His people" are the Jews, it is to be understood that the promise of the New Covenant is realized in those Jews who accept Christ. This "people" also includes those Gentiles who accept Him, and thus become "Abraham's seed": "For ye are all the sons of God by faith in Christ Jesus. For as many of you have been baptized into Christ have put on Christ. There is neither Jew nor Greek, there is neither bond nor free, there is neither male nor female; for ye are all one in Christ Jesus. And if ye be Christ's, then are ye Abraham's seed, and heirs according to the promise." (Galatians 3:26–29). We are not to neglect this blessed truth concerning the Gentiles just because the allegorizers have abused it. That the Gentiles are *in*cluded does not mean that Israel is *ex*cluded, nor is there any passage of scripture that can be so construed. God's special grace to the Gentiles in no way encroaches upon those distinctive privileges that remain inviolate for believing Israel.

God's way with Israel was to chastise them only to do them good at their "latter end" (Deuteronomy 8:16). "For thus saith the Lord of hosts: As I thought to punish you, when your fathers provoked me to wrath, saith the Lord of hosts, and I repented not: So again have I thought in these days to do well unto Jerusalem and to the house of Judah: fear ye not." (Zechariah 8:14, 15). "And it shall come to pass, that like as I have watched over them to pluck up, and to break down, and to throw down, and to destroy, and to afflict; so will I watch over them, to build, and to plant, saith the Lord." (Jeremiah 31:28). "For thus saith the Lord; Like as I have brought all this great evil upon this people, so will I bring upon them all the good that I have promised them." (Jeremiah 32:42; cf. Amos 3:2).

These particular promises cannot apply to "spiritual" Israel, understood to mean believing Gentiles. Such "spiritual" Israel did not come out from Egypt; did not wander forty years in the desert; was not dispersed into all the world; was not a curse to the Gentiles; did not so rebel against God; and was not so punished by Him.

If all this still is not enough to convince any Christian, let him read the 11th chapter of Romans and be convinced.

Part II

Christ and
the Jews:
Now

Chapter 1

Modern Arguments Against Christ

Part I served to show that no human being ultimately was responsible for the death of Christ and that Calvary was the focal point in the drama God planned for man's salvation. In Part II we deal with the various modern attempts to kill Christ by disparaging Him and His teaching. The participants here are both Jews and Gentiles, and usually are theologians who claim near-perfect knowledge of Christ, His death, and all the legal and social ramifications involved in all of life at that time.

As Jesus prayed for the original participants—so we pray for these modern participants: "Father, forgive them for they know not what they are doing."

Although Part II deals primarily with showing our Jewish brethren according to the flesh that each poisoned dart they hurl at Christ ultimately ricochets to wound the Jewish people, we believe that Gentiles likewise will profit from its reading. Our Jewish brethren's fight against Christ is doomed from the start because their weapon is falsehood, and by showing them this it is hoped that they will desist from further attempts to "kill" the Lord of Glory.

The idiotic story about the life of Christ—as circulated by rabbis in the ghettos of old—can no longer be propagated. No modern Jew would believe that Jesus performed miracles by the ineffable name of Jehovah which He stole—by some trick—from the Holy of Holies and thereby induced Jews to worship a foreign god. This scurrilous pamphlet disappeared with the ghetto.

As modern knowledge made incursions into many Jewish minds, Jewish leaders began to dispose of Christ by arguing that He never really existed and that the whole story amounts to nothing more than the figment of some visionaries' imaginations. Clever books were published to "prove" these arguments and for some time they enjoyed moderate success in convincing people that there never was such a man as Jesus. However, recent historical research and archeological discoveries leave no doubt that Jesus—the One of Whom the New Testament speaks—really lived, thus disproving the alleged "proofs" of the rabbis.

Never admitting defeat, the rabbis now have taken to the tactic of allowing that there was some such man during the Second Temple, but not exactly as portrayed by the New Testament. In other words, contrary to the assertions made by the ghetto-minded rabbis that Jesus was an extremely wicked and dangerous person, some modern rabbis have converted Jesus into a fine Jewish gentleman.

Some would even grant that He was a great rabbi.

Others would go so far as to admit that He was a great prophet, perhaps one of the greatest—but nothing more, and certainly not the Messiah. All seem to agree that He was an excellent teacher and preacher to the masses of common people—which is why they flocked to Him. Having given this much ground, many modern rabbis then immediately turn around and rob Him of any greatness—even to the point of attributing glaring moral defects to Him.

We are forced to ask just where these rabbis were able to find such a Jesus. Opposing the New Testament, which presents Jesus as a good Jew, and good man, an ideal gentleman, and as divine, the rabbis claim to have obtained knowledge from some authentic sources other than this. They have not yet disclosed where they got their information—all ancient Jewish sources present a very ugly portrayal of Jesus.

Rabbi Milton Steinberg, who is considered one of the greatest authorities on Jewish history of the time of Christ, offers insight to the liberal rabbis' "Jesus." Steinberg's opinions are those generally promulgated by Reform rabbis.

Concerning what Jews think of Jesus, Steinberg states: "To Jews, Jesus appears as an extraordinary, beautiful and noble spirit, aglow with love and pity for man, especially for the unfortunate and lost, deep in piety, of keen insights into human nature, endowed with a brilliant gift of parable and epigram, an ardent, moreover, a firm believer in the faith of his people; all in all, a dedicated teacher of the principles, religious and ethical, of Judaism." (*Basic Judaism,* page 106).

On the following page of his book, however, Steinberg reverts to the usual rabbinic teaching: "The signal fact about Jesus is that except for some relatively unimportant details which we shall specify in a moment, he propounded no ethical doctrine in which Jewish tradition had not anticipated him. Indeed, what he taught was the Jewish tradition as he had received it from Scripture and the sages. For every principle he preached, for very many of the epigrams and parables he struck off, Biblical or rabbinical precedent exists. The very phrases of the Sermon on the Mount can be paralleled one by one from the Jewish devotional literature of his time."

This latter statement is an outright falsehood—simply because there is none such existent "Jewish devotional literature" which he mentions, and there was none in existence in the time of Christ. Prayers and rabbinic literature were forbidden to be written down until centuries after Christ!

He continues: "Nor is it all true that Jesus introduced the concepts of love and compassion into Judaism that knew stern justice only. No one who considers the Old Testament can fail to perceive that ages before the Nazarene was born mercy and love had been conceived in Israel and accepted as authentic. Anyone who studies rabbinic literature will discover the ideal of humaneness preached by Jesus, far from being peculiar to him, was the common aspiration of all good souls in his people and time." (*Basic Judaism*, page 107).

After Steinberg "proves" to his readers that Jesus was neither prophet nor Messiah, he asks, "But will not the Jews accept him, if not as a prophet, then at least as a perfect man, an ideal for all to imitate? That, too, is not tenable. The sober truth is that Jesus, spiritual hero that he is, is not perfect. The ideal Jesus of the Christian imagination is actually an indealization, achieved by an unconscious, but judicious selection from New Testament incidents."

He then goes on to point out the alleged deficiencies and shortcomings of Jesus: His other-worldliness, indifference to social affairs, day-to-day living, lack of interest in the life of reason and beauty, ill-temper and chauvinism. Thus, after he has "scourged Him and nailed Him to the cross," the rabbi writes on His cross, "A GREAT MAN"—the modern version of Pilate's "I.N.R.J." or Iesus Nazarenus Rex Judaorum, Jesus of Nazareth King of the Jews.

An interesting question to put forward would be that if the "Lord's Prayer" is taken from Jewish sources, as these rabbis so claim, then why do they exert so much energy to eliminate this prayer from public schools? Several such allegations are considered throughout the remaining portions of Part II.

Another of the modern arguments against Christ is that He was not great enough to create extraordinary attention, as proved by the fact that He was not mentioned in the writings of that time.

The answer to this lame argument is that actually there was a considerable body of contemporary literature devoted to Him and to the movement which was begun by Him. There are the twenty-seven books of the New Testament—the earliest of which was written two decades after His death, and the latest near the turn of the second century. We do not know how many other Christian writings were produced in the times of the apostles, but we do know from Luke that when he took pen in hand many written accounts of Jesus' ministry already had been circulated: "For as many have taken in hand to set forth in order a declaration of those things which are most surely believed among us . . ." (Luke 1:1).

Also, there are several Christian writings that began to make their appearance near the latter part of the New Testament period, such as the Epistle of Clement of Rome, and the Didache.

Nor is evidence lacking in non-Christian sources—pagan and Jewish. For instance, there is a pagan reference to part of the crucifixion story that is dated as early as anything in the New Testament. This reference is from Thallus in Rome around the year 50. We have what Thallus said only as it is reproduced by Christian writers, who were concerned with refuting his "naturalistic" interpretation of the darkness at the crucifixion as an eclipse of the sun. An informative discussion of this reference is given by liberal scholar Maurice Goguel who, in his book *Jesus and the Origins of Christianity,* stresses its great significance in showing that the Gospel story was known in Rome, and had to be reckoned with by the intelligentsia there at an early date.

References to the crucifixion and to Jesus' miracles given by none other than Pontius Pilate would have to be dated much earlier than those above, if indeed there were such references—and that such references existed is attested to by the early Christian, Justin Martyr. Addressing his *Defence of Christianity* to Emperor Antonius Pius in the year 150, Justin Martyr invites the emperor to verify certain things about Christ by checking "the Acts which were recorded under Pontius Pilate." What Justin Martyr said cannot be verified by us today—yet, if it could not have been verified in his day he was taking a mighty big chance. If there were none such records of Pilate available to the emperor—or if available records did not contain the alleged items—Justin's case easily could have been discredited as a fraud.

There are extant references to Christ, or the Christian movement, by the Roman writers, Tacitus, Pliny, and Suetonius, not long after the turn of the second century.

Josephus, a first-century Jewish writer, also refers to Christ, and in one portion he even speaks of Christ's resurrection and miracles. This particular passage often is regarded as spurious—that is, of being "too Christian" in its wording—but this need not be of deep concern if a recent finding proves to be authentic. This finding concerns a manuscript apparently in original form, with only minor differences in wording—the differences being that the references alluded to above are in supposition form rather than statement-of-fact form. The point is that Josephus, in the first century, refers to Christ, regardless and quite independent of this contested passage. All manuscripts of Josephus' book contain this passage, and many scholars accept this passage as authentic, excepting certain words. Such eminent authorities as Adolf Harnack and F. C. Burkitt, who were not conservatives, accepted the whole passage exactly as it stands.

That even these references to Christ survived those turbulent times is a miracle of the first order. The first thing to remember is that very few people had the time, patience and skill to write books. Secondly, there were very few people who could afford to buy these books—which were hand written on parchment and thus very expensive. There may have been many books about Jesus which disappeared for one reason or another, and some still may be hidden as were the Dead Sea Scrolls until recently. Thirdly, during the wars with the Romans and the Fall of Jerusalem, most, if not all, books kept in synagogues and libraries were destroyed. The Jews who went into exile probably did not and could not take any books with them with the possible exception of the Old Testament or parts of it.

It is obvious that many current stories and biographies of Jesus existed, because we know that later the church leaders chose the four Gospels—considered as portraying the various facets of Christ and His life as sacred and authoritative—and then discarded all other similar books on this subject.

Then too, the rabbis interdicted all writings that spoke of Jesus— "That Man's" name was to be obliterated and forgotten. It became a grave sin to read a book about Jesus and all such books had to be destroyed. It is little wonder that other than the New Testament we have no books about Jesus. Indeed, there is extant no book whatsoever written in Judea at the time of Christ. The Talmud, which was finished about 400 years after Christ, mentions the person of Jesus by various names except "Jesus," whose name was not to be mentioned. Everyone who reads it, however, knows to Whom those appellations refer

If it were not for the Apocryphal books—which the rabbis rightly excluded from the cannonical writings of the Jews—we would not know much, if anything, about the Maccabees. These great heroes are not mentioned in the Talmud or in any other Jewish book accepted and sanctioned by the rabbis. The Pharisees disliked the descendants of the Maccabees and wanted them to be forgotten. The rabbis in like manner were intent on obliterating even the name of Jesus.

The rabbis, especially Rabbi Akiba, deprived any Jew of a share in the world to come who read certain "Outside Books." The books of the "Minim," usually referring to Christians, were to be burned. (Talmud SABBATH 116a).

Chapter 2

Was Christ Merely an "Innovator?"

This is a rather common charge voiced by Jewish liberals and their fellow-travellers among the Christians. Even though they may concede that Jesus was a great man, a celebrity, some sort of a prophet, an effective itinerant preacher (Maggid), a great rabbi, a talented teacher, and a capable leader of the common people, they nearly always add some reservations—claiming that He did not say anything new, and that His sayings, parables, precepts, maxims, and proverbs have been learned from the rabbis. He thus is represented as being nothing more than a good pupil who digested the words of the sages and in turn related them to the masses.

To substantiate their assertions, these people have plunged into the Talmud—which is likened to a vast sea with various streams and cross-streams wherein live all kinds of creatures—in search of words and phrases which might seem to furnish an analogy to what Christ has said. For example, they have uncovered some passages which are vaguely similar to parts of the Sermon on the Mount and some of the parables. This is done to show an easily duped world that the greatness of Jesus consisted of nothing more than the retelling to the ignorant what He heard from the great ones of the Talmud. Some liberals would begrudge Him even these virtues, and they say that many things which He retold were distorted, either purposely or through ignorance. "One must remember," they intimate, "that Jesus came from a 'hick town' surrounded by 'hillbillies.' "

To argue that Christ has not said anything new because something similar is found in the Talmud is no less ridiculous than to argue that Shakespeare did not say anything new because many things in his plays are to be found in the writings of 1972. Since the books of the Talmud were written hundreds of years *after* Christ, obviously it is impossible to prove that what is contained in these books was known before Christ—particularly when dealing with a saying of His attested to first of all by the Gospels.

The people of His time bore testimony that "Never man spake like this man." (John 7:46).

We know that it was not Christ's aim in this world to say "smart" and novel things or to entertain with interesting parables. He taught the truth and His sayings and parables were a means to this end—not an end in themselves. Apart from factors relating to His special redemptive mission, much of the truth which He taught was a reproduction of the Old Testament, applied to the circumstances in which His disciples lived. And, since the rabbis shared with Him a tradition and culture shaped by the Old Testament, it should not be surprising if their teachings had some similarities to His. But how few good grains are to be found among all that rabbinic chaff! Jesus did not say that He came to innovate, but to "fulfill"—to apply what was written according to the Spirit, rather than according to the letter "that killeth" (II Corinthians 3:6). He reaffirmed what was written, giving its quintessence and spiritual import. And of course when He referred to "what was written," He meant the Bible, the Old Testament—nothing was "written" by the rabbis at His time.

Concerning innovations, is the great commandment, "Thou shalt love thy neighbor as thyself" (Leviticus 19:18), Jewish or Christian doctrine? It generally is assumed that this is a Christian principle—the second most important in the Christian faith behind "Thou shalt love the Lord thy God with all thy heart, and with all thy soul, and with all thy mind." (Matthew 22:37–39). On the other hand, the Jews insist that this is a Jewish principle—the greatest principle in Judaism—and this contention between Jew and Christian has led to such controversy and bickering as to border on being the reverse of what this principle should be. If often seems that the self-appointed advocates of the two faiths have perverted this beautiful rule into, "thou shalt hate thy neighbor."

The truth is that the doctrine is both Jewish and Christian. The faithful believer knows that the one is the fulfillment and complement of the other. Those who endeavor to differentiate between the two should understand that properly understood—that is, as Jesus expounded it—this command is purely and simply Christian doctrine. Why? It all depends on the interpretation. According to the rabbis, the Hebrew word "R'a" (RAYAH)—generally translated neighbor—refers only to Jews. But according to Christ, who understood the Spirit of the letter, "neighbor"—that is, RAYAH—refers to every human being, whether Jew or Gentile. This probably is the reason that a certain lawyer in the parable of the "good Samaritan" asked, "Who is my neighbor?" (Luke 10:29). Apparently this was a disputed subject which needed a clear definition and Jesus, in His parable, provided that definition.

Some Jewish liberals have attacked Jesus severely for His quoting, "and hate thine enemy" (Matthew 5:43), as if this were a slanderous insinuation that the Jews teach hatred for one's enemies. These liberals justly aver that the words, "and hate thine enemy," are not to be found in the Bible. But Jesus did not say that "it was written"—He said, "ye have *heard* that it hath been *said.*" Surely they must have heard such words often from the scribes. Certain prayers in the Jewish liturgy and certain laws enacted by the rabbis against non-Jews reveal the deep hatred which the Jews—like all other peoples—always have been harboring against their enemies. This is *normal* for the *natural* man and has been since Adam fell.

In considering the two conceptions of "neighbor," we will see that the two are diametrically opposed to each other. The Christian concept is plainly set forth by Jesus in Matthew 5:43–48: "Ye have heard that it hath been said, Thou shalt love thy neighbor, and hate thine enemy. But I say unto you, Love your enemies, bless them that curse you, do good to them that hate you, and pray for them which despitefully use you, and persecute you, That ye may be the children of your Father which is in heaven; for he maketh his sun to rise on the evil and on the good, and sendeth rain on the just and the unjust. For if ye love them which love you, what reward have ye? do not even the publicans the same? And if ye salute your brethren only what do ye more than others? do not even the publicans so? Be ye therefore perfect, even as your Father which is in heaven is perfect."

According to Jesus, then, "neighbor" refers to every human being —to each of whom we owe our unrestricted love.

How different is the rabbinic concept that "neighbor" refers only to Jews. How different from the Bible passages are those of the Talmud which teach that Gentiles are excluded from all benefits of the command to love thy neighbor, and make it unlawful to save the life of a Gentile when he is in danger, to cure his sickness, to suckle his baby, or to give any aid in childbirth. It is even unlawful to give him good advice. Proof that "neighbor" refers only to Jews is found by reading from Maimonides: *Hilchoth Accum* ch. IX.16; *Hilchoth G'Neivah* ch. II.1; *Hilchoth G'Zeilah* ch. I.7; *Hilchoth Rotzeach* ch. V.3; and *Hilchoth Deoth* ch. VI.4.

The Jews likened Moses Maimonides, the greatest of the Jewish codifiers, unto Moses, the greatest of all prophets. Although one of the supposedly liberal philosophers, the Jewish luminary tenaciously stuck to all the precepts and decrees of the Talmudic rabbis, even when their words were an atrocious insult to the human race. All their discriminatory laws against Gentiles were incorporated into his code of laws. His only exception to Jewish exclusiveness was the proselyte who kept all the laws. Such an one was to be considered as "thy neighbor" and to enjoy all the privileges accorded to every Jew.

Some apologists want to explain that these stringent and discriminatory laws refer only to idolaters and not to Christians in whose midst they sojourn. This is an interesting admission, for according to Maimonides in *Hilchoth Accum* ch. IX.4, Christians *are* idolaters (see also *Hilchoth Ma'Achaluth Asuroth* ch. II.7, where Maimonides expressly states that Christians are idolaters and thus the laws regarding idolaters apply equally to Christians).

But, why should any idolater—even those of China, Japan, India, or of any of the world's jungles—be excluded from the love which we owe our "neighbor?" Whereas the Jews pray that God should destroy all idolaters, Christians erect institutions and send out missionaries to save these idolaters from the wrath of God, converting them to worship the true and living God.

To be fair to our Jewish brethren in our midst we have to assert that not only do they not observe or practice those strange laws concerning non-Jews, but with the exception of some scholars and hatemongers, they do not even know of the existence of such laws. A point in fact is that present day Jews know very little of so-called "Judaism," and they observe much less of the little which they do know. We would not have mentioned those inhuman laws if it were not necessary as an antidote to the virulent propaganda campaign of certain Jewish hatemongers who are digging into Christian writings and culling anything out of context which might indicate Christian animosity against Jews. These hatemongers are doing all they can to perpetuate the prevailing lie among Jews that most, if not all, Jewish suffering throughout history has been caused by Christ and Christian teachings. (See the author's companion book, *Anti-Semitism and Christianity*.)

There are some Jewish spokesmen who rightly contend that it is not the theory that counts, but the practice. They are saying, "What you are *doing* is speaking so loud I can't hear what you are *saying*." They are asking just where that "Christian" love is. Was it in the Inquisition? Or in the Crusades? How about the pogroms? Or perhaps it was in all the suffering and persecution which so-called Christian love has perpetrated against the Jews?

Yes, we have to admit to the truth that there are many so-called "Christians" who flagrantly have disregarded the commandment to "love thy neighbor as thyself." Those Christians and *so-called* Christians were not imbued with divine love—and many cannot rightly claim the title of Christian.

But why not take into account what has been done by *true Christian love?* This love is that which gave rise to Christian civilization and its attendant high level of general education and culture, in which institutes of mercy such as hospitals and the like which care for the destitute, and in which slavery was abolished, womanhood was elevated to the highest standard in all of history, and in which the selfless, sacrificial mission work among savage and half-savage people has transformed cannibals and head-hunters into decent, civilized people. No, this Christian civilization is not perfect—it does not yet come up to the standard of Christian perfection. But, it is the best there is in the world.

It is true that Jews have not established inquisitions, nor have they had any crusades, nor have they arranged any bloody pogroms. And, as a minority in exile they could not have done so if they had wanted to. On the other hand, can they point out any extraordinary manifestations of brotherly love? Jewish charity is exemplary—but is often merely a matter of give and take among themselves.

Nor can they attribute the atrocities of the Inquisition to *Christianity.* Those perpetrators of evil had no support or sanction for their evil deeds in the words of Christ or any other passage recorded in the New Testament.

However, they could find justification to a certain extent in the Old Testament and to a large extent in the Talmud. For example, heretic Christians and Maranos—that is, Jews who openly embraced Christianity and later returned to Judaism, or observed Judaism in secret— were burned at the stake by the Inquisition. In our modern age, we can neither conceive of nor vindicate such eccentricities of intolerance. And although such eccentricities sprang from un-Christian interpretation of God's Law, we insist they could be condoned by rabbinic law, and prove it by what Maimonides writes in accordance with a Talmudic decree: "A Noahite (a Gentile) who has become a proselyte, and been circumcised and baptised, and afterwards wishes to return from after the Lord, and to be only a sojourning proselyte, as he was before, is not to be listened to, on the contrary, either let him be an Israelite in everything, or let him be put to death." (*Hilchoth Melachim,* ch. X.3).

While we vehemently condemn the inhuman treatment of any people in general and of the Jews in particular, we must understand that the Middle Ages were truly "Dark Ages"—ages in which learning of any sort was condemned, and in which Scripture was hidden from the masses of Jews and Gentiles alike. It was a time of extreme superstition, and a time when people lived in constant fear of wars, invasions, oppressions, recurring pestilences, and so forth. People then were inhuman, and the more so in light of what the New Testament teaches.

As it serves no useful purpose to argue over who did or did not instigate the greatest number of atrocities, neither does it serve any useful purpose to squabble over who is or is not the real originator of the principle of neighborly love in human history. A better goal is for both to cooperate in propagating the command both in theory and in practice—and, of course, in mutual love, as Christ expressed it.

To close this chapter we want to give one more example of how Christ interpreted Mosaic Law according to its spirit, and this is in relation to the Sabbath rest. Jesus said, ". . . The sabbath was made for man, and not man for the sabbath." (Mark 2:27). The modern rabbis exclaim that this was not saying anything new, because something like it is to be found in the Talmud. (Again, the Talmud was written hundreds of years after Christ.) But the rabbis condemned those who violated the Sabbath laws, whereas Jesus condoned them. In fact, when He healed a man on the Sabbath, the keepers of the letter of the law wanted to kill Him: "Therefore the Jews sought the more to kill him, because he not only had broken the sabbath, but said also that God was his Father, making himself equal with God." (John 5:18).

A large volume of the Talmud deals with the numerous prohibitions on the Sabbath, the transgression of which entails severe punishment—from 39 stripes to the death penalty.

Has Christ innovated anything?

He inaugurated a new era—the era of the "Good News"—the News that every man, male and female, Jew and Gentile, rich and poor, mighty and weak, high and low—all may acquire true happiness and joy by becoming one with God.

No greater innovation is imaginable.

"Go ye therefore, and teach all nations, baptizing them in the name of the Father, and of the Son, and of the Holy Ghost: Teaching them to observe all things whatsoever I have commanded you: and, lo, I am with you alway, even unto the end of the world. Amen." (Matthew 28:19, 20).

Chapter 3

Is Christian Theology
Contrary to Judaism?

The argument here is that Christ and Christianity are too much involved and entangled with paganism and thus repulsive to Jews, who for three thousand years have been inculcated in a strict monotheism which precludes such a doctrine as the Trinity of God, which implies three gods, or of God becoming man, or the Messiah as the Son of God.

These, of course, are but half-truths: Christians indeed worship a triune God—which is not three gods. Nor is this tri-unity foreign to the Jewish religion. The Hebrew Bible—the Old Testament—abounds with the idea of the three aspects of God: God the incomprehensible, God who appears to man in the image of man, and God who communicates with man by the Holy Spirit. Concerning the divinity of the Messiah, some rabbis—such as Maimonides—denied that Messiah would be a supernatural person. Most rabbis, however, and most of the people believed that he would be supernatural—imbued with divine power and authority. These doctrines—the plurality of the God head and the divinity of the Messiah—are mentioned often in the writings of the *Kabalah* (the Jewish mystic books) as if they were part and parcel of the tenets of Judaism.

Jews and Christians both base their doctrines concerning God and His relation to man and the universe on the same Bible. Many ideas in the New Testament which seem "new" are as old as Judaism and are expressed and taught in the Old Testament. The religious life of Jesus of Nazareth was "as it was written" in the Old Testament. There was no other "Testament" in His time. The doctrines of the Plurality of God, the Incarnation, Original Sin, Vicarious Atonement, and the Deity of Christ all are based on the Old Testament.

There was no written statement of a creed which the Jew in ancient times had to recite or confess—yet it generally was taken for granted by every Jew that there was a God, a personal God Who cared for His creatures. He was aware of it, felt it, and believed it—although nowhere in the Bible was he commanded to believe in God.

Some rabbis now interpret some of the passages of the Old Testament upon which "Christian" doctrines are based as having a meaning different from the Christian interpretation. Certain rabbis began to force their own interpretations on these passages for no other reason, it seems, than to counteract the influence of Christianity. But the greatest of Jewish exegetes interpreted those passages exactly as did the Christians. The Targums, Aramaic translations of the Old Testament and which are held as most sacred besides the Bible, the "midrashim," homiletic exposition of the Bible, and especially the books of the "kabalah"—all sacred to the Jewish people—are in harmony with the Christian interpretation of those controversial passages regarding Christian doctrines.

It was in the Middle Ages that the rabbis formulated a creed which the Jew must believe in order to be a "Jew." This mainly was the work of the rabbi Maimonides (1135–1204), who formulated the "Thirteen Principles of Faith" of the Jewish religion. The first principle teaches that God is a unity and incomprehensible because there is nothing in existence to which we could compare Him, and that we cannot attribute to Him any quality, any characteristic known to man. This God of Maimonides is more like the god of the Greek philosophers and is not the God of the Bible—not the God of Israel.

As a matter of fact, Maimonides was a great admirer of Aristotelian philosophy, but at the same time was a Talmudist and he wanted the Jews to observe punctiliously all that the rabbis enacted. Held in high esteem by the Jews as one of the greatest authorities on Judaism, Maimonides taught that what the rabbis decreed was from God. But is God really one who "studies the Torah," "lays on phylacteries," "weeps over the tragic lot of His people," enjoys seeing a Jew eat matzo on Passover, is angry when a Jew omits putting on a fringed garment, or a skullcap, and other such qualities as the rabbis attribute to God? Maimonides codified these thousands of petty laws and ordinances and made them obligatory—Jews must keep them in order to please God.

Thus Maimonides has pictured for us a two-faced God: on one side He looks and acts like a good, traditional Jew; on the other side He seems to be the biggest "nothing" in the world. The unknowable deity is made into the image of a rabbi.

Maimonides' twelfth article of Faith is the belief in the coming of the Messiah. He does not indicate who the Messiah is, where He is now, whereto He will come, how He will be recognized, or how He will establish His authority.

Elsewhere in his Code of the Jewish laws, *Mishnei-Torah,* section Hilchoth M'Lachim (The Laws Concerning the Kings), chapters 11 and 12, this great rabbi specifies some identifying marks of the Messiah: "If he will be a king of the House of David and peruse the Torah, both the Oral and Written Law, as did his father David, if he will compel all Israel to keep this Torah, if he will engage in the wars of the Lord and be victorious and subdue all the nations around, and rebuild the Temple on its place, gather in all the exiles of Israel, establish universal peace and prosperity, he is the Messiah." That is what the great Maimonides decrees.

Maimonides did not like miracles. To him Judaism was in full conformity with nature, science, logic and common sense. A man possessed with common sense might want to know how this person who will suddenly come and say that he is the Messiah will be believed, how he will prove that he is the "son of David," how he will persuade the six million Jews of America, for example, to go settle in Israel, and how he will persuade the Jews to rebuild the Temple and the altars, and start anew to offer bloody sacrifices. Where will he build the Temple? Where will he get authorized, sanctified priests and Levites? How will he "force" or convince the Jews to bring sacrifices? Most Jews would scorn such rites. By what means would he secure peace over all the world? How many years will elapse before he accomplishes all these things so that he finally can prove that he is the true Messiah? Maimonides leaves his disciples in the dark!

Jews who still follow the Torah as it has been observed throughout the exile, who still are praying the three daily prayers, are reciting those "Thirteen Principles of Faith" without realizing how confused and misleading the principles are.

While the thirteen CREDOS start with the belief in an impersonal God, the Ten Commandments—the divine basis of the Jewish faith—start expressly with the personal God: "I, Jehovah, thy God have brought thee out of Egypt . . ." Rationalistic rabbis dislike the idea of anthropomorphism, and they deny the Godhead any attributes, sentiments or actions. Yet the Hebrew Bible abounds in events in which God assumes the nature of man.

How the infinite God could become finite is a mystery, but it also is an historic fact, and every believing Jew believes this mystery no less than the Christian. Why could not God, Who is omnipotent, become incarnate in the form of a human being if He so willed? There is nothing incongruous in this: "God, who at sundry times and in diverse manners spake in time past unto the fathers by the prophets, Hath in these last days spoken unto us by his Son, who he hath appointed heir of all things, by whom also he made the worlds; Who being the brightness of his glory, and the express image of his person, and upholding all things by the word of his power, when he had by himself purged our sins, sat down on the right hand of the Majesty on high." (Hebrews 1:1–3). God appeared to Abraham in the form of man and to Jacob in the form of an angel. The Jewish Bible tells of many such theophanies. Jewish liberals and rationalists would divest Judaism of all mystery and supernaturalism to contrast it with Christianity, which they aver is veiled in irrational ideas.

The Jewish Bible begins with the mystery of the plurality of God. The Hebrew word for God is ELOHIM, which is plural—"Gods." In Genesis 1:26 we read: "And God said, Let us make man in our image, after our likeness . . ." Thus God not only speaks as a plurality, but He also creates man in His own image and likeness. Does not this suggest that God temporarily may become finite—looking and acting like man? We have also the mystery of God's coming down on Sinai and the mystery of His dwelling between the Cherubim in the Tabernacle.

The Hebrew words for Tabernacle (Mishkan) and his dwelling there (Shakan) are of the same root as Shekinah (the Shekinah Glory). The word Shekinah (or Sh'Chinah) is a much-used word in Jewish lore and in common parlance. What is this Shekinah? It is a deeply veiled mystery, and it is doubtful if any rabbi could give a satisfactory definition for the word. Sometimes it means God Himself; sometimes it means some "being" other than God Himself—that is, some intermediary between God and man. The performing of certain rites, such as the laying on of phylacteries or the putting on of the fringed garment (Talith) at the beginning of the morning prayer, are preceded by a prayer for the unification of the "Holy One" and the "Shekinah." (L'shem Yichud—for the unification). This preliminary prayer contains many words hinting at mysteries which probably no Jew tries to conceive. Prayer books with English translation printed side by side leave this prayer untranslated, or the whole prayer is omitted to avoid possible questions which cannot be answered.

Adding to the mystery is the fact that while the word for God is masculine, Shekinah is a feminine noun.

Another mystery of the Jewish prayer book is a prayer which is to be recited silently at the blowing of the "Shofar"—ram's horn—on Rosh Ha'Shana (New Year), which is the most solemn of the Jewish rituals. This prayer—which is difficult to translate clearly—invokes the intercession of "Yeshua (Jesus) the Lord of the FACE" (Sar-Ha'-Panim). Modern liberal rabbis claim that this prayer was interpolated by Christian printers. In most recently published prayer books this mysterious prayer is omitted entirely.

This "Lord of the Face" is a Biblical concept. It was the "Face" which struggled with and blessed Jacob. (See Genesis 32:25–32). In Exodus 33, God promised Moses that His "Face" would go with him: "And he said unto him, if thy FACE go not with me, carry us not up hence." (Exodus 33:14, 15. See also verse 19). The English translation here is "presence" for the Hebrew word "Panim"—but Panim literally means "Face." It is the Angel mentioned in Exodus 23:20. It is the "Angel of His Face" (presence, in English) that saved Israel: "In all their affliction he was afflicted, and the angel of his FACE saved them; in his love and his pity he redeemed them; and he bare them, and carried them all the days of old." (Isaiah 63:9). The Psalmist praises God for the help of "His Face" (here the English is "countenance"): "Why art thou cast down, O my soul? and why art thou disquieted in me? hope thou in God: for I shall yet praise him for the help of his FACE." (Psalm 42:5). In the Sanctuary there was a "Table of the Face" and on it the "Bread of the Face" (in English, "shewbread"). (See Exodus 35:13; Numbers 4:7; Deuteronomy 31:17). "I will hide my face from them . . ." Many exegetes identify this FACE with the "Angel of the Covenant" (Malachi 3:1).

It is neither incongruous nor foreign to Judaism. There is the mysterious SATAN in the Jewish Bible, and there are the mysterious "fallen angels." (Genesis 6:4). Christianity has received such doctrines from the Jewish Bible. Curiously enough, the ancient sages explained ". . . the Spirit of God moved upon the face of the waters" in Genesis 1:2 as meaning the "Spirit of the Messiah." (See Ba'al ha'Turim, the commentary which usually is printed with the commentary of Rashi in the Five Books of Moses).

Rashi—revered by Jews as the greatest commentator on the Bible —being aware of the various revelations of God to man in diverse forms, and in commenting on the first commandment, says that it comes to emphasize that all those appearances (theophanies) are one and the same God. (Rashi on Exodus 20:2).

That the Godhead is a plurality is known throughout the Hebrew sacred literature, but it always was reiterated that the various *forms* are not various *Gods* but are *One*. For example, we read in the *Zohar,* the most sacred Kabala-book: "The mystery of the word Elohim, the word used in the Hebrew Bible for God, or Gods, is that there are three degrees, each distinct by itself, yet all one; joined in one; not separable from one another." (*Zohar* on Leviticus 29:4).

Another example of how modern rabbis differ from the ancient rabbis, who generally interpreted the Bible in the way Christian exegetes have done, is the word "Shiloh" in Genesis 49:10. Christian exegetes attribute this word to the Messiah, suggesting that Jesus, as the Messiah, perpetuated the kingdom of Judah through the House of David. Otherwise, Jacob's prediction would be false. Modern rabbis, to contradict the Christian interpretation, deny that Shiloh has any reference to the Messiah, and they propose a different interpretation as we shall see later.

Now the *Targum* of Onkelos paraphrases this verse (49:10) as, "The scepter shall not depart from the House of Judah, nor a lawgiver from his descendents till the Messiah will come, whose is the Kingdom, whom the nations will obey." Rashi also refers Shiloh to the Messiah, as does the *Targum,* and he explains why this word is used to signify the Messiah. *Ba'al Ha'turim* shows that the numerical value of the Hebrew Letters in Yavo Shiloh, "the coming of Shiloh," is equivalent to the numerical value of Mashiach (Messiah). So also are the numerical values of Shiloh and Moshe (Moses) the same, suggesting a prophet like Moses.

These three expositions of the Pentateuch—the *Targum,* the commentary of *Rashi,* and *Ba'al Ha'turim*—usually are printed on the same page as the texts and all three always have been kept sacred and authoritative by the Jewish people.

Modern liberal rabbis scoff at the idea of a suffering Messiah, and say that if there be a Messiah at all—which they also deny—he should be triumphant. Since Jesus was defeated, he could not have been the true Messiah. When confronted with Isaiah 53, these modern liberals claim that it refers to the suffering Jewish people. Contrary to these rabbis' assertions, all great Bible exegetes treat this chapter as referring to the Messiah, as do Christians. For example, Rabbi Moshe El-Sheikh says, "Our Rabbis with one voice accept and affirm the opinion that the prophet here is speaking of the Messiah."

Now let us examine one of the most solemn prayers recited at the Day of Atonement service: ". . . Our Righteous Messiah has turned His face from us: horror has seized us and we have none to justify us.

He has borne the yoke of our iniquities, and our transgressions, and is wounded because of our iniquities, and our transgressions, and is wounded because of our transgression. He beareth our sins on His shoulder, that He may find pardon for our iniquities. We shall be healed by His wounds, at the time the Eternal will create Him (the Messiah) as a new creature. O bring Him up from the circle of the earth—to assemble us the second time . . ." This remarkable prayer, although the wording is not quite clear, obviously cannot mean anyone else than the suffering Messiah as depicted in Isaiah 53. Only perverted casuistry can apply Isaiah 53 to the people of Israel who indeed were suffering, but not silently without protest and for the sins of others. They certainly were not suffering willingly as was the person referred to in that chapter.

To explain the apparent discrepancy of a suffering Messiah with other prophecies relating to a triumphant, ruling Messiah, Jewish lore has invented two Messiahs: "Messiah, son of Joseph," who is to be defeated and die; and "Messiah, son of David," who is to rule over all the world forever.

Modern rabbinical critics may not agree with those "old-fashioned" interpretations of the Bible. However, the traditional exegesis is the only "Judaism" which the majority of the Jewish people throughout the ages have accepted. Thus, pure, unadulterated Judaism has basically the same theology as has pure, unadulterated Christianity— the two are in harmony.

Another alleged contradiction between Christian theology and Judaism is that the Jew, unlike the Christian, feels no need of a mediator between himself and God—he has direct access to his Father in Heaven. Such is the general claim of the so-called "liberal" rabbis who are so vociferous in demanding that we expurgate the New Testament of passages which they do not like. They would, if they could, do the same with certain Old Testament passages.

Indeed, if they had their way, very little of the Jewish Bible would be left intact. The whole book of Leviticus would have to come out; also the greater part of Exodus, especially that which contains God's ordinances about the priesthood, sanctuary, altars, and the various sacrifices. These gentle modern rabbis "see red" when they read about "blood." They cannot bear the sight of blood nor its smell, but it is there in the Bible—the Jewish Bible. That blood starts with Abraham, the father of the Jewish people: "In the same day the Lord made a covenant with Abraham . . ." What occurred on that memorable day? On the behest of the Lord, Abraham performed certain "bloody" rites of which, we are sure, the rabbis would not approve. (See Genesis 15:18). God, that is the God of Israel, both approved of it and commanded it.

Why did God want a special abode where He could dwell? Why did He want certain particular persons, the priests, to have access to Him in His sanctuary? These persons, too, could come to Him only after having performed certain rites, usually involving bloody sacrifices. Why? We do not know. We know only that the God of Israel ordained these "irrational" ordinances of mediation and vicarious atonement as the very warp and woof of the Hebrew religion to represent the fundamental truth that man can come into the presence of the holy God only when his sins are covered—thereby foreshadowing what became a reality in the cross of Christ.

Since the cessation of the ordained sacrifices following the destruction of the Temple in Jerusalem (70 A.D.), all Jewish prayers invoked several times daily are focused on the restoration of the sacrifices which ceased "because of our sins."

Contrary to modern liberal rabbis, the orthodox Jewish religion still recognizes the need of priestly mediation by the ordained rites of sacrifices, in accordance with such examples of mediation as described in I Samuel 7:8, 9 and elsewhere in the Old Testament.

Thus, Christianity is based on this same mystic Jewish principle in holding that Jesus by His supreme sacrifice is the perfect sinless high priest, who mediates between man and God. (See Hebrews 9:11–15).

Of course, every Christian has free access to the Father. The one prayer that Jesus Himself taught His followers, on the other side of the cross, is directed to the Father in Heaven, but—standing on this side of the cross—it is natural and in accord with the New Testament for us to implore the Father in the name of the Son, Who has atoned for us and made us fit to approach the Throne of Mercy.

The Jews, being aware of man's unworthiness to come before the holy Almighty God, ask God to hear their pleas for the sake of their patriarchs—Abraham, Isaac and Jacob—with whom He made an everlasting covenant. The Jews often have resorted to the mediation of saintly people and even dead relatives in their graves have been asked to intercede before God to bring succor in some special need. No, mediation, or intercession, is not a Christian innovation. It was innovated by the Jewish God, as it is recorded in the Jewish Bible.

Chapter 4

Is Christianity a Morbid Religion?

With this allegation, Christianity's so-called "other-worldliness" is taken to task. Jewish critics often picture Christianity as a gloomy, dismal, melancholy religion and point out that Christ Himself admitted that His kingdom is not of this world. It is intimated by these critics that Christianity teaches that the main objective of every human being should be Heaven—the "other world." They say that Christianity teaches that man ought to suppress the flesh, stifle all natural desires, and live an ascetic life—that we should feel the burden of guilt for "original sin."

The critics even resort to the misleading argument of using the monasteries, convents and celibacy of the "Christian priests" as proof of how Christianity is divorced from the realities of life.

There is need, in the above allegations, to adhere strictly to some facts—pertinent facts regarding traditional, orthodox Judaism, and facts that often are ignored or glossed over by these critics. In all his waking hours throughout all his life the traditional, orthodox Jew is chained to laws and customs. Not only his actions, but also his every thought is restricted by a "do" or a "do not," a "thou shalt" or a "thou shalt not." He is always apprehensive lest he commit some transgression or forget some command and thus suffer severe retribution in this life, or be condemned to the fires of hell after his death. The greatest part of his three daily prayers are imploring God to bring him back to the Promised Land whence he was driven from because of his sins and where the sacrifices could be reinstated. He is always to mournfully bear in mind the destruction of the Temple.

While considering allegations of Christianity's "worthlessness" because of its "other worldliness," we are wont to ask: "Why do all the traditional, orthodox Jews endeavor to be 'good Jews'—that is, to keep the law and do good—if they do not hope to have a share in the 'other world'—the 'world to come?' " How then is Christianity any more other-world-minded than is the hope of "Olam ha'Ba" (the world of bliss) which has kept the traditional Jew alive? It is true that some Jews today speak less of "Olam ha'Ba"—but those Jews have abandoned Judaism as their way of life. The observant Jew has prayed three times a day, every day, for the establishment of the Kingdom of God. He learned in *Avoth* (Wisdom of the Fathers) that this world is only a vestibule before the "world to come," and man is to prepare himself here in order to enter the Hall—that is, "paradise." (*Avoth* 4:21). *Avoth* reminds him that man is nothing, that he had an unsavory beginning and has dust as his ending.

The alleged "morbidity" of Christianity also is a result of the doctrine of "original sin" as promulgated by Christ's followers. So claim our detractors, the Jewish critics. This doctrine, which makes man feel that he is a lost creature, that he is inherently wicked and fallen from grace, and that he can be saved only by the Grace of God through the atonement provided by the blood of Christ, degrades the human being and frustrates his hopes and desires to be good and make good on his own. Following this line of reasoning, the modern liberal rabbis expect to prove themselves as the champions of the human race as a whole and as staunch defenders of the dignity and uprightness of the individual human being.

It is their contention that the doctrine of "original sin" is incompatible with Judaism, and therefore must be rejected by the Jewish people. They posit that this doctrine is the evolutionary base from which the other Christian notions proceed, including the idea that the flesh is evil and must be suppressed, and that all life in this world is worthless, vain and futile. All that man should do is to hope, pray and wait for the Kingdom of Heaven—for a legendary world to come some day, and in the meantime there is no use striving, aspiring or trying to ameliorate things. It is no use to resist evil—it is better to turn the other cheek to bullies, tyrants and despots—and Christians should not try to enjoy life in this "valley of tears." According to the picture thus painted by the rabbis, Christianity is a system of morose, gloomy, anti-social brooding which impedes the progress of civilization and the improvement of the human race.

In juxtaposition to this "morbid," "frustrating" Christianity, the rabbis place Judaism as a luminous, joyous religion which encourages man to grasp out of life all its blessings and pleasures, and improve it more and more so he may live and enjoy it more and more.

If these liberals spoke in their own name we would have no quarrel with them. But they claim to represent and to expound Judaism and we, as do most Jews, contest their claim to represent Judaism and especially their right to interpret Judaism. These ostentatious, vociferous protagonists have radically changed and mutilated Judaism beyond recognition, and then quote Scriptural passages torn from proper context in an attempt to substantiate their notions of what Judaism is, or should be.

According to the Scripture portions they quote, everything God created was good, including man. Man was created in the image of God and God blessed him; therefore he must be inherently good. If he ever sins it is an exception to the rule and he can ask for and obtain an easy forgiveness. God is a compassionate, forgiving God and man does not need any mediator nor any "blood" to appease his God. Man is quite self-sufficient and has a steady, immediate and free access to God his Father. In other words, if we were to believe these rabbis, we might think that man still is in the Garden in Eden. They obviously are ignoring Genesis 3:23, 24: "Therefore the Lord God sent him forth from the Garden of Eden, to till the ground from whence he was taken. So he drove out the man; and he placed at the east of the Garden of Eden Cherubims, and a flaming sword which turned every way, to keep the way of the tree of life." No, man forfeited this Garden of Eden long, long ago.

To discuss the merits or shortcomings of "original sin" is not within the scope of this book. Our purpose within the confines of this book is to show those rabbis   who know little of Judaism and even less of Christianity—that the doctrine of "original sin" not only is compatible with Judaism, but also is part and parcel of Judaism. Christians neither invented this doctrine nor any other doctrine—they inherited this and other doctrines from Judaism, the Judaism of the Holy Bible, the Jewish Bible. This is the Judaism bequeathed to them by their own God.

While it is true that the passages so quoted by the rabbis are well known and implicitly believed by every Christian, it equally is true that Christians know what followed the early blissful period in the Garden of Eden, as it plainly is recorded in the Bible. The Bible—which is the center and circumference, the Alpha and the Omega of Judaism—clearly states that man was created in the image of God and received God's blessing; but then goes on to record that man soon disobeyed God's will and fell from His blessing. Consequently, God cursed him and condemned him to continuous tribulation culminating in death, and even repented that He had created man. (Not even the rabbis can deny that man dies, after suffering a great deal, or that life is an almost continuous struggle for existence frought with many hard knocks and frustrations.)

Contrary to what modern rabbis teach, the Bible—the Jewish Bible—conspicuously speaks of man's sinfulness and his fallen estate, and this opinion of man's fall also is often expressed in post-Biblical Jewish literature—especially in its liturgy.

It is true that Judaism has never formulated any doctrines to be recited and confessed orally from time to time. There was no need for defining articles of faith and putting them into writing, because these basic concepts generally and implicitly were believed by all Jews. For example, there was no need to orally confess a belief in God, or the coming of the Messiah, or the resurrection of the dead, and so forth—they were just believed. Among the doctrines believed by Jews from Moses' time until the present day is the doctrine of "original sin." This may be substantiated by referring to and quoting from some of the many passages in the most cherished and revered sources and personalities of Judaism.

The Pentateuch—the most sacred book of Judaism—was written by Moses as dictated by God Himself. This book is recited in weekly portions at the synagogue on Sabbath Days and Feast Days. Small portions of it are recited in congregations on Mondays and Thursdays.

In this book we read: ". . . the imagination of man's heart is evil from his youth." (Genesis 8:21). Rashi, the greatest commentator of the Bible, explains this verse thus: when the child emerges from his mother's womb, the evil spirit, or inclination, is implanted in his heart. Rashi apparently based this statement on the Talmud: *Sanhedrin* 91b and *Nedarim* 32b state that the "Yetzer ha'raa"—the Evil Impulse (to sin)—begins immediately after birth.

"And God saw that the wickedness of man was great in the earth, and that every imagination of the thoughts of his heart was only evil continually. And it repented the Lord that he had made man on the earth, and it grieved him at his heart." (Genesis 6:5, 6).

Concerning the curse which rests upon man: "And he called his name Noah, saying, This same shall comfort us concerning our work and toil of our hands because of the ground which the Lord hath cursed." (Genesis 5:29).

That man inherently was evil we learn also from the story of the flood. Man became so evil that God had to destroy him, leaving only Noah and his family who found grace in the eyes of the Lord. Of man's sinful estate we read all through the Bible in stories similar in their condemnation of man—for instance the narrative on the tower of Babel, Sodom, and the like.

The Jewish people were not any better—their sinfulness began with their beginning as a people and continued all through their history until their exile. Soon after witnessing that greatest of all revelations on Sinai they had a golden calf made for themselves. Moses and the prophets who followed him often had to rebuke them for their rebelliousness against God: "Ye have been rebellious against God from the day that I knew you." (Deuteronomy 9:24).

The Psalter has been a "Vademecum" of every Jew, a boon companion all through exile and an inexhaustible source of comfort and consolation to the people as a whole as well as to the individual in all his trials and tribulations. Many Jews know all of the 150 Psalms, or most of them, by heart. A great many of the Psalms are incorporated into the daily prayers.

Now let us see what this most sacred, revered and cherished Jewish book has to say about man. According to this book of Psalms, by the "sweet singer of Israel," man is inherently sinful. We read in Psalm 51, verse 5: "Behold, I was shapen in iniquity; and in sin did my mother conceive me." In a preceding verse (3) of the same Psalm he says: "My sin is ever before me." Then (verse 10) he implores God: "Create in me a clean heart, O God; and renew a right spirit within me." If he wanted a clean heart created in him, does that not mean that his heart was naturally unclean? Speaking of man, in Psalm 53, he says (verses 2 and 3): "God looked down from heaven upon the children of men, to see if there were any that did understand, that did seek God. Everyone of them is gone back: they are together become filthy; there is none that doeth good, no, not one."

Further examples of man's fallen estate and of his "nothingness" are provided in Psalms 39:5, 6; 49:20; 62:9; 89:46; 130:3; 134:3, 4 and others. A true picture of man is painted in Psalm 90, which is called the "Prayer of Moses."

The *Siddur,* or prayer book—the most Jewish of Jewish books—reminds the Jew several times a day that he is sinful and that he needs God's grace to wipe out his sins and the sins of his fathers. Furthermore, through these prayers he acknowledges the need of sacrifice for atonement and his main prayers are an invocation that God will bring him back to the "Promised Land" where the sacrifices can be reinstituted. Just how sin-conscious the Jews really are may be learned from their attempts to alleviate the punishment of their departed relatives by reciting certain prayers, and studying certain passages of the Talmud, and by distributing alms and kindling special candles on Yahrzeit (memorial day of the departed).

Contrary to the teachings of the "reformers"—that God dispersed His people among the Gentile nations so that they might teach them the Torah—the Jews repeatedly confess in their prayers that it was "because of our sins we were exiled from our land." Concerning the "reformers" teaching we must ask just when and how have the Jews fulfilled that so-called commission? Only Jewish Christians have done such a thing as this "commission" would require, but the rabbis either ignore this fact or condemn it.

In addition, there are several other Biblical and post-Biblical Jewish books that teach this doctrine of man's sinfulness and lowliness—the same doctrine which the "Modernist" rabbis claim to be foreign to the Jewish heart and mind.

Answering the allegation of the morbidness of Christianity, we should understand that although the Christian believes in man's sinfulness, he does not bear its burden of guilt. On the contrary, he rejoices in the divine assurance that his sins have been washed away by the blood of Christ, and that he now is pure and stays *at one* with God, the "Holy One of Israel."

Christianity is HAPPINESS. While the Jewish prayers as a rule are expressed in fear and awe, accompanied by sighing, weeping and sobbing (especially by women), the Christian's prayer is exultant, jubilant and triumphant! No unbelieving Jew can experience the happiness felt by the true Christian as he sings:

"Blessed Assurance, Jesus is mine;
Oh what a foretaste of glory divine"

or:

"Joy to the World, the Lord is come!
Let earth receive her King"

or:

"Jesus is all the world to me;
My life, my joy, my ALL"

Yes the Christian is happy because he knows that he is released from the guilt of sin—original sin and all other sins—and he has divine assurance that his sins are forgiven. He does not fear death, as Jews usually do, nor does he fear hell—the Christian knows that he is redeemed by Christ and thus is at one with God. "These things have I spoken unto you, that in me ye might have peace. In the world ye shall have tribulation: but be of good cheer; I have overcome the world." (John 16:33). ". . . and, lo, I am with you alway, even unto the end of the world. Amen." (Matthew 28:20).

The Christian is aware that life in this world is only fleeting, temporal and accompanied by temptations and tribulations, as the Bible—the Jewish Bible—points out; but he does not neglect the life which God has given him. Jesus Himself was an example of how to improve life, to ameliorate suffering, and to make life pleasant. He fed the hungry, healed the sick, entertained at a wedding party, comforted the lowly and dispensed happiness all around. Where in non-Christian countries can one find such wonderful institutions founded to advance mankind in learning, art, health and comfort as one finds in countries that have been nurtured by Christian influence?

True Christianity is the precise opposite of morbidity.

Chapter 5

Alleged Shortcomings of Christianity

Among the various shortcomings and deficiencies which the modern rabbinic experts allude to in Christianity are "ignorance" and "superstition" and their boon companions "intolerance" and "persecution." They point to the fact that throughout His ministry Jesus associated with the poor in spirit, the ignorant—and they quote Him as saying, "Blessed are the poor in spirit," to prove their point. The rabbis of His time already had called attention to this fact, as we are told in John 7:48, 49. His special predilection for children was, so it is charged, because of their ignorance, and attention is directed to ignorance in the countries where the "church" exerts much influence—usually in reference to certain Catholic countries.

We are not going to defend the Roman Catholic Church nor explain why in certain countries where it dominates the cultural life that many of the people are illiterate and superstitious. That sector of the church departed from the very basics of Christianity soon after its inception some 1,400 years ago. We could retaliate by saying that where the rabbis dominated the life of the Jews, as they did in the ghettoes and small towns, the Jews were quite ignorant, superstitious and intolerant. No book other than the sacred books of Jewish law were opened to the Jew and he was not permitted to attend any school except the Talmudic schools—which instructed him only in the ways of Judaism with its many trifles and absurdities.

It was not "ignorance" which Jesus liked, but open-mindedness, humility and innocence. If He showed some preference for the common people it was to raise their morale—which the rabbis, the learned men, endeavored to suppress and degrade. The rabbis hated and despised the "Am-ha'-ARETZ" (the uneducated plain folks), but Jesus loved them and found them more receptive than the so-called elite.

He went about teaching the masses because He wanted them to know the "truth which would make them free." Christianity does not foster ignorance and does not preclude natural science, etc., as proved by the fact that the great majority of schools—primary, secondary, college, etc.—and other cultural institutions in the "Western" world have been founded and maintained by Christians. As a matter of record, most of the modern cultural institutions in Asia and Africa also have been established either directly by Christians or indirectly through Christian influence.

Modern critics claim that Christianity was born and nurtured in superstition and point to New Testament reports of miracles—in which "only superstitious people can believe"—such as Jesus' encounter with Satan, and His exorcizing of evil spirits. In addition, they refer to a long list of foolish practices of "Christian" people in the past and some even in the present.

Truth and freedom are not compatible with superstition. The simple fact is that Christians are the least superstitious people in the world. The little superstition which may exist among them is not "Christian" and has absolutely nothing to do with faith in Christ. The Christian's acceptance of miracles and supernatural occurrences mentioned in the New Testament is not superstition, but a belief in the wonderful ways of God with man.

For the modern rabbis to ridicule this belief is tantamount to treating the Old Testament and the rabbinic writings and teachings in exactly the same manner. Not only do the rabbinic books, such as the Talmud, abound in really superstitious things, but the Bible—that is, the Old Testament—contains many occurrences which we do not quite understand but which nonetheless are true and which seem superstitious to unbelievers. From A to Z, the Jewish religion is based upon the miracles which God has performed—and most of them were performed in connection with Israel.

But according to the line of reasoning of the modern rabbis, as used against Christianity and the New Testament, the Old Testament is nothing more than a collection of superstitious and immoral tales. This precisely is the judgment of Gentile infidels—the so-called "higher critics" who in reality are "higher anti-Semites." These "wise" liberal rabbis need to realize that the Old and New Testaments will either stand together or fall together. (For a discussion at length on this topic, see the author"s companion book, *Anti-Semitism and Christianity*.)

Satan, demons and evil spirits are as much a part of the Old Testament as they are of the New. For example, Satan appears in the first two chapters of Job, an evil spirit possessed King Saul in I Samuel 16, and Saul consulted a spiritualist "medium" named Endor.

The rabbis of Jesus' time and afterwards believed that He performed miracles—but they ascribed His supernatural power to being aligned with Beelzebub: "Then was brought unto him one possessed with a devil, blind and dumb: and he healed him, insomuch that the blind and dumb both spake and saw. All the people were amazed, and said, Is not this the son of David? But when the Pharisees heard it, they said, This fellow doth not cast out devils, but by Beelzebub the prince of the devils. And Jesus knew their thoughts, and said unto them, Every kingdom divided against itself is brought to desolation; and every city or house divided against itself shall not stand: And if Satan cast out Satan, he is divided against himself; how shall then his kingdom stand? And if I by Beelzebub cast out devils, by whom do your children cast them out? therefore they shall be your judges. But if I cast out devils by the Spirit of God, then the kingdom of God is come unto you." (Matthew 12:22–28).

A short while later the rabbis ascribed His extraordinary power to the miraculous ineffable name of God, which He stole from the Holy of Holies. The main point is that all through their existence the Jews have believed in miracles. It was this belief that kept the Jewish people alive in spite of all the attempts, throughout their long history, to destroy them. The Jew himself is a living and everlasting miracle.

We challenge the rabbis to explain the high cultural standards of Jewish communities in Christian countries and the low standards of culture, the ignorance and superstition of Jews living in non-Christian countries.

We challenge the rabbis to prove their allegations wherein they associate Christianity with intolerance and persecution. Of course there have been many cases of intolerance, injustice and persecution perpetrated by people who were called "Christians." In no case, however, can such acts be ascribed to Jesus or to His true followers—those who *rightly* name the name of Jesus. Jesus the Christ preached love, equality and brotherhood between human beings. He did not hate even the Pharisees—however much He rebuked them—any more than did the prophets hate their own people when they rebuked them throughout Old Testament times. In no case did Jesus incite the people against the Pharisees or the other leaders—He taught the people to respect those who sit in the "seat of Moses." Jesus urged the people to observe all that the Pharisees preached, even though the Pharisees themselves did not practice what they taught.

There is nowhere in the New Testament the slightest hint, or suggestion, or encouragement of hatred or persecution of any human being, no matter who he is, what he is, or what he has done! There is the noblest example of love, compassion, and pardon shown by Jesus even to the worst of sinners. He offered His life for them, one and all—there is no greater love than this.

Chapter 6

Is the New Testament Anti-Semitic?

The instrument used most often by "Christ-killers" is the argument that Christ inaugurated the era of anti-Semitism with its associated hatred and persecution of the Jews, and that the New Testament propagates anti-Semitism as no other book in history. They claim that in addition to being a pagan book, the New Testament is the main textbook of anti-Semites, and attribute all the suffering experienced by Jews throughout their tragic history to it. Jews have been indoctrinated with the deep conviction that as long as this book exists Christians will hate and persecute them.

It is for this latter reason that there has been so much protest from Jewish quarters against teaching the New Testament in public schools in the United States. It is for this reason that some of the Jewish leaders have been so adamant in their efforts to have Christendom delete all "anti-Semitic" passages from the New Testament—especially the story of the trial and death of Christ. In this latter effort they have been joined by Christian Philo-Semites, liberal ministers, infidels, "friends" of the Jews, and the like—none of which have any semblance of an accurate concept of what the New Testament really teaches.

Rabbis ignore the fact that the Jews had been hated and persecuted for 1800 years before Christ came to the earth and that they have been persecuted wherever they lived in non-Christian countries. The rabbis shut their people's eyes to the fact that only in Christian countries have the Jewish people survived all suffering. They persistently and repeatedly point out all the isolated incidents of persecution the Jews had to endure in Christian countries. Untiringly they point to the Inquisition, the Crusades, the Pogroms, and the various other atrocities by which the "Christians" endeavored "to destroy the Jews."

It is true that wicked, sinful persons have taken the Lord's name in vain and perverted His words to persecute not only the Jews, but also other people including "dissident" Christians, but one must not blame God when someone takes His name wrongly. The Jews have not been the only victims of such perversion of God's name and God's Word, as evidenced by the infamous Inquisition and equally infamous Crusades. Instead of being examples of Christian hate towards the Jew, as the rabbis claim, these mad criminal actions took the lives of more Christians than of Jews, and all supposedly in the name of the Lord.

Nevertheless, anti-Semites—whether mere hatemongers or actual murderers of Jews—could not then, cannot now, nor will be able in the future to cite any word or passage from the New Testament as justification for their evil deeds and designs. As we already have pointed out, there is not even one word in the New Testament that might indicate in any manner, however slight, that Jesus wished or permitted anybody to hate or punish any human being for whatever he had said or done.

We also should remember that despite occasional eruptions of hate and persecution, the Jew has preferred to live in Christian countries, or in non-Christian lands which were governed by Christians.

Peaceful co-existence has been the rule between Jew and Christian and whereas the Jew prospered and persecution was the exception in Christian countries, the opposite has been the case among non-Christian countries, such as Islamic lands. We cannot emphasize strongly enough that evil-doers, whether they are called "Christian" or not, are *not* followers of Christ—they are followers of Satan.

The New Testament is considered by the whole world to be the best book that the Jews have ever written. It is one of the greatest tragedies in the tragic history of the Jewish people that this most Jewish book— the most philo-Semitic book—has been so badly maligned by many of the Jewish leaders.

If the Jewish leaders were not so blinded by unreasonable hatred, they would not so gullibly follow in the footsteps of anti-Semites who by various slight-of-hand tricks "detect" passages in the New Testament which "sound detrimental" to the Jewish people. If these leaders would harken to common sense, to reason, and to truth, they would do all in their power to frustrate the obvious evil intents of anti-Semites. This they could do by elucidating those so-called "detrimental and deleterious" passages which the anti-Semitic forces always cull out of context and misinterpret, and by showing the world that the New Testament is full of admiration and love for the Jewish people. They would show that the New Testament is in harmony with Christ, who so loved His people that He chose to live with them, minister to their temporal and spiritual needs and finally to lay down His life for them. Then they would be able to show the world that Christ even forgave those few Jews who plotted His death and who delivered Him to the executioners.

The New Testament has proclaimed to every nook and corner of all the world that there is a Jewish people, that this is God's Chosen People, that salvation is of the Jews (John 4:22), that to the Jews were the promises and oracles of God given, and that to the Jews were God's prophets and His own Son sent (Romans 9:3–5). Just how "Jewish" the New Testament is—in the best sense of the word—even a cursory reader may see right from the beginning of Matthew 1:1 through Revelation 22:21.

The first verse of the book of Matthew begins with the words that tell to all who have ears to hear and eyes to see that Jesus was the son of David, the son of Abraham—the two most beloved persons in Jewish life and thought.

Should Satan prevail and the narrative of the trial and death of Jesus be eliminated, the world would be without the Jesus who suffered, and bled, and died, and rose from the dead. It would be without the Christ, the Saviour Who atoned for it, as emphasized in John 3:16. That really is what the modernists want, however. They would let their particular "Jesus" live in memory as a fine, fictitious man, a pretty legend, a fairy tale, a subject for students of folklore and nothing more. Their clever arguments are being propagated extensively among Jewish people as well as in Christian colleges and universities.

Then Satan will have achieved one of his goals through the anti-Semites because without Jesus there would be no inspired, divine Bible, neither Old nor New Testament, and the Jews will have been deprived of being a God-privileged people—thus, with no claims to a "Jewish" land, or of any special regard whatsoever. Then the Jews will find themselves not only in pagan countries, but in a pagan world with no hope of survival for any length of time.

Mark, the second book of the New Testament, opens with the words, "The beginning of the gospel . . . as it is written in the prophets." What prophets? He takes it for granted that everybody knows that these were the Jewish prophets—there were no others.

Luke, the third book, commences the story of Christ with a certain saintly priest—a Jewish priest—who, while ministering in the Temple of the Lord, was promised by a special messenger of the Lord to have a son who would be the precursor of the Messiah—the Messiah of the Jews. Some time later an angel of the Lord came to a certain maiden—a Jewish maiden—and announced that she would bear a son who would inherit the throne of David His father and would reign over the house of Jacob forever. (See Luke 1:26–34).

John, the fourth book, tells in the very beginning that Jesus came unto His own (John 1:11)—meaning the Jews. John also tells us of the first man who recognized Christ in His true being, the "Lamb of God." That first man also was a Jew (John 1:29). The first man who bore witness to the Messiahship of Jesus as the One of whom Moses and the prophets spoke was a Jew (John 1:46). The first man who recognized and confessed Jesus as the Son of God, the King of Israel, also was a Jew (John 1:50). John also quotes Jesus as affirming that salvation is of the Jews (John 4:22).

It is obvious that the four authors of the Gospels, Matthew, Mark, Luke and John, all were Jewish-minded and certainly not anti-Semites as some Jews accuse them. From these four writers all the world has learned that Jesus was JEWISH, just as Moses and the prophets expected Him to be.

In addition to these four writers, the greatest and most venerated men in the Christian Church are the two Apostles Peter and Paul. Both were true Jews and both preached and practiced "to the JEW first." Neither blamed the Jewish people for their share in the death of Christ because both of them knew that those who participated in the "killing" of Jesus did not know what they were doing. Both taught that the death of Jesus was so planned by God the Father. Both loved their people. Peter told them, "Ye are the children of the prophets, and of the covenant which God made with our fathers, saying unto Abraham, And in thy seed shall all the kindreds of the earth be blessed. Unto you first, God having raised up his Son Jesus, sent him to bless you, in turning away every one of you from his iniquities." (Acts 3:25, 26).

Paul so loved the Jews that he was willing to be accursed from Christ for their salvation. In spite of all the tribulation that he suffered at the hands of his brethren the Jews, he persistently went to the Jews first. Of his love and admiration for the Jews we read: "What advantage then hath the Jew? or what profit is there of circumcision? Much every way. chiefly, because that unto them were committed the oracles of God." (Romans 3:1, 2). Again: "For I could wish that myself were accursed from Christ for my brethren, my kinsmen according to the flesh: Who are Israelites; to whom pertaineth the adoption, and the glory, and the covenants and the giving of the law, and the service of God, and the promises; Whose are the fathers, and of whom as concerning the flesh Christ came, who is over all, God blessed for ever. Amen."

In our ministry, from hundreds of pulpits and through hundreds of articles in Christian periodicals, we have quoted such passages to show Christians how Jesus and His followers loved and esteemed the Jewish people. Jewish leaders would better serve their people by making good use of such passages in the New Testament than by endeavoring to find some semblance of anti-Semitism and enlarging and distending it to gigantic, horrifying dimensions.

The Jew-baiters who have distorted passages in the New Testament would easily have found a multitude of other excuses for their maniacal hatred and persecution even if the New Testament was not in existence. The use of New Testament passages culled from context has been a matter largely of convenience. For instance, Pharaoh, Haman and others had some "good" reasons for wanting the Jewish people exterminated—long before the New Testament came into being. Apion, the Egyptian against whom Flavius Josephus wrote a book of refutation *(Contra Apion)*, was a "great" anti-Semite. What he wrote against the Jews in his day is almost as modern as today's anti-Semitic diatribes, and Apion never had read the New Testament and never had heard of the crucifixion.

In three issues of the *Southern Israelite,* a Jewish publication, it was written, ". . . anti-Semitism is deeply imbedded in the New Testament . . . Thus Rockwell is . . . as Hitler was—a product of Christian dispensation, which has taught babes in Sunday Schools that the Jews killed their saviour . . ." (August 17, 1962). Again, ". . . It was not (the murder of six million Jews) within a Moslem world or a pagan world that the fiendish butchery took place. It was in Christian Europe and by butchers nurtured in Christian homes . . ." (December 14, 1962). And, ". . . All persecution of Jews, all pogroms, the Spanish Inquisition, have their mainspring in the mystery surrounding Golgotha . . ." (January 4, 1963). Poisonous articles of this nature have appeared from time to time in various Jewish publications, and indeed, such charges are almost universal among the Jews throughout the world.

We have written to the editors involved on many occasions calling their attention to the fact that such articles might cause great harm because every Christian reading or hearing of them would profoundly resent such defamatory lies. We have begged editors to correct the harmful impressions readers would get from such false statements. We wanted their readers to know that Hitler and most other anti-Semites were notoriously anti-Christian—no less than they were anti-Jewish—that Jews were persecuted in non-Christian countries, and long before Christ, and that Jews could not be killed in large numbers in avowedly non-Christian countries for obvious reasons. For instance, in Moslem Saudi-Arabia—a land almost as large as all of Europe—not a single Jew has been killed in hundreds of years. Of course, no Jew has been allowed to live there throughout these hundreds of years, which has some bearing on the statistic. History bears out the testimony that when Hitler's vile government took control of Germany, all Christian influence was suppressed and that in the most brutal methods known to man.

Our letters to these editors generally were ignored.

These articles appear periodically in the various Jewish publications and are damaging to all concerned—especially to the Jews themselves. The Jewish critics are well aware that the New Testament will not be mutilated according to their dictates, but they are satisfied in that they are quite successful in instilling a poisonous hatred in the hearts of many Jews against Christianity.

In contrast to these critics, one of the greatest geniuses of the Jewish race had this to say about Christ as known from the New Testament: "The pupil of Moses may ask himself whether all the princes of the house of David have done so much for the Jews as that prince who was crucified on Calvary? Has not He made their history the most famous in the world? Has not He hung up their laws in every temple? Has not He vindicated all their wrongs? What successes did they anticipate from their Messiah? The wildest dreams of their rabbis have been far exceeded. There is one fact which none can contest. Christians may continue to persecute Jews and Jews may persist in disbelieving Christians, but who can deny that Jesus of Nazareth, the Incarnate Son of the Most High God, is the eternal glory of the Jewish race?"—Benjamin D'israeli (Lord Beaconsfield).

Indeed, Jewish survival after the destruction of Jerusalem was possible only through the influence of the New Testament. There are few Jews where there is no New Testament. The more a people is influenced by the New Testament, the better it treats the Jews in their midst. The establishment of the State of Israel was made possible mostly—if not solely—by the help of New Testament-influenced people. The State of Israel has thus far maintained its position thanks to Christian people, and when its enemies—all non-Christian peoples—would attack it, only Christian people would come to its rescue. Of all

people in the whole world, only those people who have been influenced by the New Testament believe that the Jews have a right—a
legitimate claim—to the land which they call the "Land of Israel."

If the rabbis could accomplish the impossible task of destroying the
New Testament or its influence, they would *ipso facto* destroy the only
friendship that Israel has. Only the New Testament Christians believe
in the "God of Israel" and that He promised the "Land of Israel" to
the "People of Israel." Only New Testament Christians believe that
that land belongs to the Jewish people by divine right, and to New
Testament Christians "divine right" is the most valid, most incontesta-
ble, and most incontrovertible right.

The Talmudic sages said that the Second Temple was destroyed
because of "hate without cause." (Talmud *Yoma* 9:6). Will the modern
"Christ-killers" destroy the third, the present commonwealth, because
of their modern hate without cause? God forbid!

It is our prayer and hope that the Jewish people—who still are God's
own people and forever will remain so—will turn their backs on the
false shepherds and turn their faces to the True Shepherd.

Chapter 7

Are Jews Ignorant
of the True Christ?

The great majority of the Jewish people today know as little about Jesus—the true Jesus, Jesus the Christ—as do the pagans in distant lands who have never heard the Gospel preached. It is strange that Jews living for the most part in Christian countries, who meet Christians day by day, see Christian churches and diverse other Christian institutions, and who hear of Christian activities and festivals, know practically nothing about the author and originator of all that is called Christian civilization—the very civilization in which the Jews always have preferred to live, in spite of its real and imagined shortcomings.

Missionaries working among the Jewish people often hear such cynical remarks as: "I don't believe in the Father, why should I believe in the Son?"; or, "I do not believe in the Old Testament, why should I believe in the New Testament?"; or, "I don't believe in Moses, why should I believe in Jesus?" Although stated cynically, these comments express the present religious condition of the Jewish people as a whole.

There is not much difference between these and the attitudes and religious conditions of the people in the time of Jesus: "For had ye believed Moses, ye would have believed me: for he wrote of me. But if ye believe not his writings, how shall ye believe my words?" (John 5:46, 47).

Humanly speaking, there have been two main reasons for this ignorance of the true Christ. The first is that He has not been preached to them in power: "How, then, shall they call on him in whom they have not believed? And how shall they believe in him of whom they have not heard? And how shall they hear without a preacher? And how shall they preach except they be sent? As it is written, How beautiful are the feet of them that preach the gospel of peace, and bring glad tidings of good things!" (Romans 10:14, 15).

The second is that their leaders have misled them: "As for my people, children are their oppressors, and women rule over them. O my people, they who lead thee cause thee to err, and destroy the way of thy paths." (Isaiah 3:12). And, "For the leaders of this people cause them to err; and they who are led of them are destroyed." (Isaiah 9:16, and see also Ezekiel 34).

Throughout the past 1900 years whenever the leaders saw, suspected or imagined a danger of the people turning toward Christ, they immediately employed all possible means to avert that danger. Holding to the precept that "the end justifies the means," they have used malicious and unjustifiable methods in their campaign against Christ, including severe persecution of those Jews who confessed belief in Him. While Jesus was on earth the leaders succeeded somewhat in infusing doubt, suspicion and animosity in the hearts of the people against Him. One such tactic was to attribute His miracles to the power of Satan (Beelzebub), and another was to accuse Him of sedition, that is, instigating the people to open rebellion against Rome. (See John 11:47–50).

After the resurrection of Jesus and the destruction of Jerusalem and the Temple some years later, there seems to have been a great awakening in the spiritual life of the Jewish people. Thousands recognized Him "Whom they have pierced" (Zechariah 12:10) and in rapidly increasing numbers they turned to faith in Jesus the Messiah. This of course alarmed the rabbis who considered Jesus as an imposter, a seducer and a sinner who had been condemned to death and lawfully executed by the Sanhedrin. In addition, they were concerned by the influx of Gentile proselytes who became "Jews" without observing the traditional Jewish Law (Christians at that time were considered as a Jewish sect), and considered it a most serious threat to Judaism.

Furthermore, while a large number of the people still cherished the hope of liberation from the Roman yoke, and while preparations were being made to rebel and overthrow the Roman rule, the believers in the Gospel of Christ would have nothing to do with that hopeless attack on mighty Rome. They could not believe in a false Messiah, such as Bar Kochba, because they knew Jesus was the true Messiah, the One who conquered death and whose return in power and glory they expected daily.

Such were the causes of the rabbis' assault against this new cult, the "minim." "Minim" usually referred to the believers in Christ, but it sometimes included any heterodox sect. The main objective was to have the "minim" excommunicated—that is, expelled from both the synagogue and the Jewish community—and special prayers of imprecations against the dissidents were incorporated into the three daily divine services. The reading of the Gospels was prohibited upon pain of losing a share "in the world to come" (meaning "Heaven").

Thus did the rabbis of the first and second centuries succeed in building up an almost impenetrable wall of partition between the main body of Jewish people and those who believed in Christ.

During the dark Middle Ages came the possibility that many Jews would turn to Christianity to escape persecution—it was decidedly more advantageous to be integrated into the Christian environment. Many other Jews were inclined to embrace Christianity out of genuine conviction and for many good reasons. Many Jews wondered why God permitted His people to suffer so much, and they wondered why the expected Messiah tarried. Questions such as these could be answered only by the faith that this Jesus is "the One of whom Moses and the prophets spoke."

Attempting to avert this danger, the rabbis concocted a tale which presented a sinister, baleful and horrible image of Jesus, showing Him to be the archfiend and the enemy of the Jewish people and of the Jewish Religion. In this gruesome tale Christ was portrayed as a vicious magician who possessed tremendous power through the use of the ineffable name of Jehovah, which he stole from the Holy of Holies in the Temple. Although caught and put to death by the great rabbis, this magician still wielded enormous power with which to harm the Jews. Besides being the god of the Gentiles—whom he taught to hate and persecute the Jews—he also was flying about once each year on Christmas in search of Jewish souls. (The author remembers how on Christmas day the Jewish "Cheder"—elementary school—children huddled together in the synagogue in fear and trembling, lest he—"That Man"—might pounce upon us and snatch the souls of one or more of us.) He seldom was mentioned by the name of "Jesus"—usually He was called "That Man" or the "Goysher god" (the god of the Gentiles), and other scurrilous designations.

This squalid, ludicrous and puerile tale—known as "Toldoth Yeshu" ("Biography of Jesus")—was handwritten and secretly circulated in the ghettos during the Middle Ages. It served quite well as a powerful deterrent to Jews contemplating desertion from the Jewish camp and who thought of going over to their enemies and their abominable deity.

The rabbis succeeded in alienating Jesus from the masses of the people—which they had been trying to do since His baptism at the hands of John. Although these leaders no longer could kill Him—the One who conquered death—they managed to "kill" His name, His claim, and His fame, at least in so far as the Jewish people were concerned. This kind of "killing" continued throughout the Middle Ages and into modern times. Today's Jewish attitudes toward Jesus are the end result of this "killing"—not of the supposed "rejection" of Jesus during His time on earth, nor of God's supposed "rejection" of the Jewish people as a result of their "rejecting" Jesus when He came to them. As we already have shown in earlier chapters of this book, neither of these "rejections" has foundation in the Word.

As the European people emerged from the Dark Ages—triggered by the Renaissance and the Reformation—the Jewish people in their midst also were granted the opportunity to emerge from their dark ghettos. When they came out and looked around, the first thing they learned was that their ghettos really were *dark,* and not only physically dark, but what is worse, they were spiritually dark. They discovered that an oppressive darkness degraded and enslaved the Jewish spirit within its walls.

Among the many other things, traditions and prejudices they felt had to be discarded was that rank, rehashed hodge-podge, that ridiculous and damaging tale about Jesus. No newly enlightened Jew could give any credence to that disgraceful farce. The new danger faced by the rabbis, then, was that the people who had found the old tale discredited now would want to know the true story of Jesus. The knowledge of the true story was in fact proving fatal to "Rabbinism," because thousands of Jews were turning to the newly discovered Jesus. New stratagems were not long in coming in their constant battle against the truth, and new methods of crucifying Christ quickly were devised.

The new stratagem—their new crucifixion—is more dangerous than the former attempts, mainly because the new attacks against Christ are intended to be total and universal. The former assaults against Christ mostly were internal—mainly to alienate the "apostate" Jew (Jesus) and to deter Jews from believing in Him. With the threats to Judaism inherent in the enlightenment, they not only endeavored to save Jews from Him, but also to "save" the whole world from Him. Part of the new strategy was (and is) to have Christians renounce and repudiate their faith in Him and in the New Testament, and thus "kill" Him with no possibility of a resurrection as an aftermath. (It is interesting to note the parallels that modern infidels falsely claiming the name Christian have drawn to this line of reasoning.)

The Jewish people now are standing at the parting of the ways in their long and tragic history. They are asking themselves, "Whither?" The "dry bones" are beginning to stir and there is a marked eagerness on the part of the average, intelligent Jew to learn and to know the right way. Large numbers in Israel have turned to the Bible—to the sacred words of the ancient prophets—and many have turned to the New Testament in their search for the truth, ignoring the 1900-year ban on this Book. Already many are beginning to recognize Jesus as the One of whom Moses and the prophets spoke—and the rabbis do not like this serious new threat to "Rabbinism." The means they employ to crush and suppress these new trends are dangerous to all concerned—Jew and Gentile alike.

Our intention in writing this book and for dispelling the ignorance of the true Christ is because we are convinced that when Jewish people are saved, they will become the greatest promulgators of the truth. We are convinced of this because we know the teaching of the Bible and because we know the Jewish people and their potentialities.

Chapter 8

Do Hebrew Christians
Cease to be Jews?

Many Christians today wonder why the Jewish leaders so persistently endeavor to discredit Christ and His teachings in the hearts and minds of the Jewish people. Christians reason that while there might have been some basis for combating Christ during His lifetime, surely now after His resurrection and after He "fulfilled what was written"—that is, after He proved His Messiahship—it is time for the Leaders to realign their thinking. Now, after Jesus inaugurated a new era, a new reckoning of time; after He changed the image of mankind and as civilized nations abandoned idolatry with all the abomination and horror that were an integral part of it; after the creation of what now is called "Christian civilization" with its institutions, cultural and humanitarian achievements, and the like—all these coming as a consequence of that once rejected Nazarene (Christ)—is it not past time for Christians to ask that the Jews reconsider and reexamine the nature and merit of that Man whom the whole world regards as the greatest Jew in all of earth's history?

Of course the answer to this question, at least in so far as we consider the Jewish people as a whole, is that "blindness in part is happened to Israel until the fulness of the Gentiles has come in." (Romans 11:25 and see also Acts 15:15, 16 and I Corinthians 12:12, 13).

Nonetheless, we should try to understand the reasons behind the hostile attitudes of present day leaders. Although we find it questionable, we can feel sympathy with the leaders' argument that a Jew who adopts Christianity ceases to be a Jew and thus becomes an irreparable loss to the Jewish people—who already have suffered so many catastrophic losses. This argument leads us to ask: "Who is a Jew—and by what identification marks may one be recognized as a Jew?" The answer to our question has been and is being searched for by many scholars and religious leaders around the world, and the more so since the birth of the modern State of Israel. And, although many of the greatest Jewish leaders have proposed an answer to the question, no practical definition has thus far been derived.

The current state of the question rests upon two proposed definitions by two opposing sections of the Jewish people—the religious and the national.

While the religious leaders hold that the Jewish religion is what makes a "Jew," the nationalists claim that race is what makes a "Jew," and neither theory abounds with consistency. To the religionists, a Jewish citizen of America is nationally an American of the Jewish religion, etc., and to the nationalists one born of a Jewish mother is a Jew even if he does not observe the Jewish religion. The religious theory states, however, that he remains a "Jew" even if he does not adhere to the Jewish faith—he ceases to be Jew only when he adopts another religion. And, according to the nationalists, a Jew born of Jewish stock ceases to be a Jew if he believes in another religion, although he does not and cannot by any means change his race—his ancestors.

This confusing bit of mental gymnastics over semantics is based on the Jewish antagonism and dread of "another religion"—that is, of Christianity, because Jews do not "convert" to any other religion. For example, it is doubtful whether the Reform rabbi or the nationalists would be much concerned about a Jew who becomes a Shintoist or Confucianist—both the religionist and the nationalist still would consider him as a Jew for all intents and purposes.

This fear of Christianity is not now based on superstition, as formerly was the case, and the spokesmen of both the religious and nationalist camps are cultured people who would resent being called superstitious in their views and concepts. In considering this fear, we must examine the objections of both the liberal rabbi and the nationalist.

The liberal rabbi is the most active in combating Christianity and is apprehensive that the modern Jew will convert to Christianity if he is not prevented and hindered by all possible means. He knows that Judaism, of any type, has lost its attraction and its importance to the cultured and enlightened Jew of today.

A great part of the negative attitude towards Judaism may be ascribed to the teaching and preaching of these liberal rabbis. For many years they have glorified Judaism as a "rational" religion, as contrasted to "irrational" Christianity (as we saw in an earlier chapter). They present Judaism as a religion of deed, as opposed to creed, and even assert that a Jew does not have to believe in any dogma—not even in the existence of a God. By "deeds" the Reformers do not refer to the "irrational" rites of ancient Israel, such as the sacrifices, the observing of dietetic laws, the antiquated rituals of marital life and the numerous laws relating to strict observance of the Sabbath. No, all that "Judaism" means to these liberals is to be good to one another, to love each other, to practice the Golden Rule and to observe the Ten Commandments.

One of the Scriptures they quote to substantiate this interpretation of Judaism is Micah 6:8: "He hath shewed thee, O man, what is good; and what doth the Lord require of thee, but to do justly, and to love mercy, and to walk humbly with thy god?" In addition, they quote from the Talmud to this effect, and what they have done is to re-form, or transform, the Jewish religion into a simple code of ethics acceptable to every human being. Thus, the average Jew reacts by saying, "If this be so, why adhere to a system called 'Judaism?' Why not be just a decent citizen? Why pay dues to rabbis and Temples? Why be different from Gentile fellow citizens?"

The average Jew also is calling into question the self-segregation—the isolation and detachment from non-Jewish neighbors—which entails a great deal of self-denial and casts a shadow of mystery upon the Jew that makes people suspect and even dislike him. All these adversities really are self-inflicted, and that because the rabbis insist that in order not to kill, or steal, or bear false witness, or be bad to fellow men, one must be a Jew. Many a Jew wonders why he must pay such a high price for the privilege of being called "Jew," and wonders why he should not relinquish his burdensome heritage and become a fellow man and citizen without being set apart. Nor does he know any good reason why he should not intermarry, why he should keep away when his neighbor celebrates his holidays, why he should avoid invitations to Gentiles' homes, why he should not eat non-kosher food with his neighbor, nor why he should not be amalgamated and welded with the other inhabitants of the same community.

Nor are the liberal rabbis ignorant of these attitudes. They have come to the realization that nothing can keep the Jew within the fold of "soul-less" Judaism—neither imposing Temples, erudite sermons, special social activities, nor special entertainments have revitalized interest in Judaism. Unable to make Judaism attractive, they apparently have decided to make the outside world—that is, the Christian world —as unattractive and unappealing as possible, and thus have opened a campaign in America against Christ and Christianity. This reminds one of the woman in the story of King Solomon, who decided to have the child killed—reasoning that if she could not have it then so no one else could have it either.

The nationalists' objection to conversion is based solely on the fear of the loss to Judaism of a Jew who adopts Christianity. Their argument is that the Jewish nation already has lost about one-third of its number—six million out of eighteen million—to the horrible Nazi onslaught, and that now every single Jew is dear to the nation. A Jew being converted means that he and his descendents are lost forever to the nation.

It unfortunately is true that a Jew who professes belief in Christ does indeed become lost to the Jewish nation—but this is not the fault of the convert. He does not "cut his ties" with his people, rather it is his people who cast him out.

Jewish intolerance toward a convert to Christianity has no parallel in any other nation.

If the Jews could tolerate converts—as do the Irish or Danes, or Hindus, or Swiss, or French and other nations—the Jew who adopts Christianity would remain among his people, and his children and children's children would remain nationally Jewish. There would be no loss whatsoever to the Jewish people. They would be a certain faction of the people—for example, as are the Sephardic Jews, the Yemenites, the Karaites, the "Bene Israel," the Chasidim, or the Neturei-Karta, who from the national point of view are a real blight on the people.

This is as it was in the beginning. For long years after the time of Christ, the Jews did not contest the right of their brethren who confessed Him to be called "Jews." Although disliked, as were the other sects, Jewish Christians were simply considered as one more sect—as faulty, erring Jews—but Jews nonetheless.

National Jewish intolerance toward the convert recently has been demonstrated by the Israeli Supreme Court against a certain "Brother Daniel," who was as good a Jew as a Jew could be, but with one fault—he confessed belief in Christ. He was declared to be not a Jew.

Here we have seen the reasons for the modern attitude, and we have seen that it is a poor reason. Now it is time for the Jewish people, who have begun to shake off the fetters of medievalism and spiritual slavery, to shake off old prejudices and hatred for Christ and hatred for those Jews who adopt Christ as the Messiah. It is time to let these Jews remain Jews within the fold.

Chapter 9

Is There a Cure for Israel?

Yes, there is a cure for Israel and it is to be found by diligently searching the Scriptures, the Bible—the Jewish Bible—as did those Jews at Berea: "These were more noble than those in Thessalonica, in that they received the word with all readiness of mind, and searched the scriptures daily, whether those things were so." (Acts 17:13). Jesus Himself urged the people to search and study the Scriptures: "Search the scriptures; for in them ye think ye have eternal life; and they are they which testify of me. And ye will not come to me, that ye might have life." (John 5:39, 40). The Scriptures referred to in both cases are Moses and the Prophets—there were no other Scriptures in their day.

Forgetting those things which are behind, our Jewish brethren (according to the flesh) should ask the question that thousands of Jews asked Peter after hearing him preach (Acts 2), "What shall we now do?" Today's answer to this question remains exactly the same as that given by Peter almost two thousand years ago: "Repent." Repenting of sins and refusing to be led astray by liberals of various sorts who deny the existence of sin is the Scriptural cure for Israel. Our Jewish brethren today should not be beguiled by the traditional leaders into believing that they have nothing to learn from the goyim (Gentiles), or that the Jews are better than any other people. These statements are put forth by the leaders in an effort to blind the people to the truth which long has escaped them.

Whether or not the Jews are better than others, or whether or not they have anything to learn from others, does not matter in the least. The Jews were chosen to be a special people, "God's people," and totally subservient to God's will. Whether or not the Jew is good enough by human standards does not matter, for surely the Jew is not worse than other peoples. The fact is that neither the Jew nor any other people is good enough in the eyes of God. The Jew is not as God intended the Jew to be, and this point is proven by the frequent rebellion against the will of God as recorded by Moses, the first and greatest of Jewish prophets, and as recorded later by all the true prophets.

Moreover, Moses and the other prophets predicted that the Jew would be driven out of the Promised Land because of their sins, and this precisely is what happened. In their prayers, the Jews recognize this retribution for their sins. Nor have they fully repented of this sin—else all the Jewish people now would be peacefully settled in the Promised Land as the prophets also predicted. The last faithful leader and true shepherd of Israel at the beginning of the second Temple was Nehemiah, and today's Jew would do well to read what Nehemiah thought of the Jewish people, and today's Jewish people should take his words to heart—and thus disregard what modern liberals, the false leaders, say today.

The repenting done thus far by the Jews obviously has not been efficacious. One way remains, and that is the only way—the way that Peter told his listeners: "Repent, and be baptized every one of you in the name of Jesus Christ for the remission of sins, and ye shall receive the gift of the Holy Ghost." (Acts 2:38). No matter how strange this may sound, no matter how shocking to the average Jew of our time, it sounded quite reasonable, quite Jewish, when Peter said it to the Jews of his time. There is no other way, there is nothing else that will avail but to repent, "Shuvu!"

Our Jewish brethren should beware of self-appointed spokesmen who perpetuate hate and prejudice against Jesus the Messiah. It is true that some of them mean well, that some of them are earnest in their zeal for God and the Jewish people, but this zeal is without proper knowledge. It also is true that others speak out of a malicious heart, and it is true that neither group tells the truth about Jesus—they all mislead.

The prophets long ago saw the danger of false leaders: "For the leaders of this people cause them to err; and they that are led of them are destroyed." (Isaiah 9:16). "As for my people, children are their oppressors, and women rule over them. O my people, they which lead thee cause thee to err, and destroy the way of the paths." (Isaiah 3:12). "Woe unto the pastors that destroy and scatter the sheep of my pasture! saith the Lord." (Jeremiah 23:1). "Thy prophets have seen vain and foolish things for thee; and they have not discovered thine iniquity, to turn away thy captivity; but have seen for thee false burdens and causes of banishment." (Lamentations 2:14). "Son of man, prophesy against the shepherds of Israel, prophesy, and say unto them, Thus saith the Lord God unto the shepherds: Woe be to the shepherds of Israel that do feed themselves! should not the shepherds feed the flocks?" (Ezekiel 34:2-8).

The only ray of light throughout the dark history of the Jews is the new State of Israel. This too is in grave danger of being overwhelmed by powerful enemies, and perhaps would be without the direct intervention of God—as manifested in three major wars of survival. Except for Christians, this new Jewish State has no friends on the face of the earth—and these Christian friends are being alienated by direct and indirect attacks against Christianity by some of the Jewish spokesmen.

Moses predicted the Israelite's evils and troubles, and also predicted the only cure for them. The cure obviously is not in vociferously clamoring that "we are God's people," that "we are teaching the world the true religion." Neither is there any merit in the erection of imposing buildings, synagogues and Jewish centers because God rejects all such shallow and worthless worship: "Wherefore the Lord said, Forasmuch as this people draw near me with their mouths, and with their lips do honour me, but have removed their hearts far from me, and their fear toward me is taught by the precept of men." (Isaiah 29:13). "And they came unto thee as the people cometh, and they sit before thee as my people, and they hear thy words, but they will not do them: for with their mouth they shew much love, but their heart goeth after their covetousness." (Ezekiel 33:31). "Nevertheless they did flatter him with their mouth, and they lied unto him with their tongues. For their heart was not right with him, neither were they stedfast in his covenant." (Psalm 78:36). Jewish history amply demonstrates that they seldom followed the true and faithful shepherds—the false shepherds were more appealing to them.

Not only did they hinder Christ from teaching the true service of God, but they also hindered His disciples and apostles after Him from promulgating His truth. They have decried, maligned, disparaged, banned and persecuted any Jew who has dared to state even the slightest particle of truth about Christ. Even in our enlightened and democratic era they have harangued and harassed the great Jewish author, Shalom Ash, for writing favorably about Christ. Great American rabbis, such as Stephen Wise and many others, have been maligned and severely criticized for telling some truths about Christ. Even the great Hebrew scholar, Klausner, was harassed as one who "sold his soul to the missionaries" because of his book *Jesus of Nazareth,* which refutes the obsolete and ridiculous stories about Christ, as well as the writings of certain liberal Jews who have claimed that Jesus never existed.

Today's Jewish leaders should bear in mind that Israel is a holy people, God's own people, temporarily estranged from God because of their sins. They should be seeking to reconcile the Jewish people with their God: "Cry aloud, spare not, lift up thy voice like a trumpet, and shew my people their transgression, and the house of Jacob their sins." (Isaiah 58:1 and see also Micah 3:8). Today's leaders should emulate the true leaders of ancient Israel, such as Moses, Samuel, Zerubbabel, Ezra, Nehemiah, and the Maccabees, who feared neither kings, nor priests, nor false prophets—nor public opinion as a whole. (see Deuteronomy 1:17.)

The cure for Israel is prescribed by Hosea 3:5 and 6:1: "Afterward shall the children of Israel return, and seek the Lord their God and David their King; and shall fear the Lord and His goodness in the latter days . . . Come and let us return unto the Lord: for he hath torn, and he will heal us; he hath smitten, and he will bind us up." And, again: "And I will pour upon the house of David, and upon the inhabitants of Jerusalem, the spirit of grace and of supplications; and they shall look upon me whom they have pierced, and they shall mourn for him, as one mourneth for his only son, and shall be in bitterness for him, as one that is in bitterness for his firstborn." (Zechariah 12:10).

Then it will come to pass ". . . that as ye were a curse among the heathen, O house of Judah and house of Israel; so will I save you, and ye shall be a blessing: fear not, but let your hands be strong." (Zechariah 8:13). "And the remnant of Jacob shall be in the midst of many people as a dew from the Lord, as the showers upon the grass, that tarrieth not for man, nor waiteth for the sons of men." (Micah 5:7).

We would suggest that Christians who sincerely and earnestly wonder why the Jews today reject Christ should differentiate between "Jews" and "the Jews." The Jews as a nation do not accept Him because of some inscrutable mystery, of which Paul gives us a glance into in Romans 11:11 (see also Matthew 13:11). In the fulness of time they will accept Him, as Paul carefully explains in Romans chapters 9 through 11, and as Zechariah records in 13:6.

Concerning individual Jews, we maintain that they have not "rejected" Him nor do they "reject" Him. "Reject" implies "to throw away," or to throw back what has been offered, and the fact is that Christ has not yet been properly presented to the Jews as He should have been during their long exile.

When Christ preached to the multitudes, thousands responded and came to Him. When Peter preached to them about Christ, thousands more responded and came to Him. And so it was with the other apostles, and so has it been through the ages that whenever Christ has been sincerely and lovingly preached to Jews, many have responded. Alas! After the time of the apostles and early missionaries, very little about the true, gentle, loving, forgiving Christ has been preached to the Jews. "How then shall they call on him in whom they have not believed? and how shall they believe in him of whom they have not heard? and how shall they hear without a preacher?" (Romans 10:14).

The great Jewish writer, Israel Zangwill, once remarked, "Had Christians handled us with Christlikeness, there would not be a single Jew in Europe." Rarely have the Jews met Christians who have exhibited to them the Spirit of Christ. Rarely has Christ been presented to them intelligently, sympathetically, and convincingly. On the contrary, most so-called Christians, animated by prejudice and animosity, have by their un-Christian conduct embittered and estranged the Jews from any consideration of accepting Christ as their Savior. This sinful relation between Christian and Jew must be changed.

We would ask the reader: "Have you personally presented Christ to them? Have you helped those who endeavor to preach Christ to them?"

Finally, you are your brother's keeper—you are commanded to preach the Gospel "to the Jew first." All you have to do is to sow the seed; some of it will fall on good ground and bear good fruit, and some of it will be wasted—but our command remains the same.

What About a New
Trial for Jesus?

Some 2,000 years ago Jesus stood before the highest court of Justice of the Jewish nation—on trial, charged with the violation of certain Jewish laws. An hour or so later this trial was transferred to the Roman ruler who convicted Him of the charges, sentenced Him to death and soon executed Him. This single trial and execution had a more formidable impact on the history of mankind than any other single event apart from creation itself.

All civilized nations of that time accepted Jesus as the Savior of the world, and in the course of time this execution led to what now is known as European or Christian civilization, of which every white man is justly proud.

But that trial had its detrimental effects—mainly upon the Jews because as a people they had believed that their supreme tribunal had tried and convicted Him in strict accordance with Jewish law.

Consequently, ever since that trial there has been friction between Jews and the Christians who surrounded them. This friction often has led to horrible atrocities being perpetuated against the Jew.

From time to time Jewish writers have come out with a plea for the Jewish people to re-try the case of Jesus, based on "strong evidence" that His judges were corrupt and biased and that the entire proceeding of the trial was not in strict accordance with Jewish law. We have proven that this is false reasoning, but it still prevails today.

These writers have been convinced that a re-trial by authoritative, prominent rabbis will exonerate Him and thus He will be accepted as a true and faithful brother.

All such demands for a new trial have been either disregarded or flatly rejected for two main reasons: first, the bias and hate against "that man" Jesus has been too ingrained in the Jewish heart to permit such a consideration; and second, there has been no Jewish supreme tribunal during the 1,900 years the Jews have been in exile.

However, since the Jewish (sovereign) State of Israel has been reestablished, these two factors hindering the convening of a new trial have disappeared. Through the last few decades the implacable bias against and hatred for the Jews has diminished, and now a Jewish supreme court of justice has come into being. And in view of this favorable change, many Israelis would welcome such a retrial.

Recently a well-known and highly skilled lawyer thought the time had come for this revision. In Jerusalem—the city where Jesus was condemned to death—this lawyer urged the supreme judicial authorities to review the charges brought against Jesus and the manner in which the trial was conducted. For ninety minutes he argued the case for his client, showing that the entire procedure "was a tragic miscarriage of justice. The trial was not conducted in accordance with due process of law, and Jesus was sentenced by a Roman court which was prejudiced against the Jews." Thus the lawyer argued that the present Supreme Court ought to exonerate Jesus of all charges brought against Him.

The court rejected his application, however, and said that Jesus reputedly was sentenced to death by the Roman government of Judea which is equivalent to a sentence handed down by a foreign military tribunal. Therefore, the court held that there is no sufficient reason for present-day judicial authorities to take up the matter.

Not content to be silenced by his first failure, the lawyer stated that he would try again in the future.

We would like to add that whether or not a modern court tries this case again, history has proven beyond the shadow of a reasonable doubt that He is the pure, immaculate, sinless Lamb of God Who took away the sins of man. It is our fervent hope and prayer that the Jewish people soon will recognize Him to be what He truly is. The original trial was legal and proper and was necessary in God's plan for our redemption. "Search the Scriptures . . ." and you will find, and know, the Truth.